More Praise for *The Disciplined Leader*

"I absolutely recommend this book to leaders in all fields. John Manning and MAP really zero in on the essentials of leadership. You will create and see fantastic results!"
—David Emmett, Senior Vice President, Conservation International

"Manning's easy and concise fifty-two-lesson format will direct any leader to the Vital Few things that will make an enormous difference."
—Roland Spongberg, President and CEO, WKS Restaurant Group

"Most companies have talented employees, but the successful ones are able to keep everyone focused on the same vision. That vision has to be reiterated by senior management regularly. John Manning has laid out how in a superb way."
—Don Johnson, Vice Chairman, former President and CEO, and founder of American Business Bank

"As a CEO, ask yourself the following question: How effective is the transmission mechanism for your vision to employees? If you commit to the process in this book, you'll soon see the strategic alignment you found so elusive is actually very obtainable."
—Joseph Panebianco, President and CEO, AnnieMac Home Mortgage

"Whether you're looking for tools that help manage accountability or need your leadership team to tackle tough business challenges, *The Disciplined Leader* can help you get better results *faster!*"
—Chris Hardeman, Vice President of Sales, Act-On Software

"Everything is important to owners and executives, but it takes a lot of discipline to put aside the less important things. *The Disciplined Leader* helps you concentrate on your Vital Few."
—Jesus Cardenas Jr. and Jose Cardenas, Senior Vice Presidents, Cardenas Markets

"It's all too easy to get lost in the onslaught of information and decisions that characterize a leader's day. John Manning helps you cut through the noise and zero in on the things that are the most vital for you."
—Lori Gangemi, CEO, AbilityFirst

"Being a great leader requires focus on the things that matter and the discipline to hold yourself accountable. In *The Disciplined Leader*, John Manning encourages leaders who want to lead their team to greatness and keeps them focused on the Vital Few—the most important things."
—Craig S. Nelson, Chairman, Nelson Family of Companies

"*The Disciplined Leader* provides advice in fifty-two brief chapters that are crisp, clear, and actionable. This book is a must-read for young career-minded high performers as well as seasoned leaders looking for ways to fine-tune their game."
—Tim Psomas, Chairman of the Board Emeritus, Psomas

"*The Disciplined Leader* gives the invaluable wisdom that comes from experience—it's the go-to tool for a leader at any level."
—Steve Distante, CEO, Vanderbilt Financial Group

"*The Disciplined Leader* will become a useful tool for your business, enabling you to identify and prioritize the vital factors that will allow you to manage and grow your business."
—Robert Curry, CEO, Alamitos Enterprises (Jiffy Lube franchisee)

"Few of us are born leaders. For the great majority it is a constant learning and growing experience. John Manning carefully defines what it takes to be a dynamic leader and offers a pragmatic and effective process to become one. *The Disciplined Leader* is a must-have for anyone who is serious about being effective and passionate about inspiring others."
—Albert J. Zdenek Jr., President and CEO, Traust Sollus Wealth Management, LLC

"*The Disciplined Leader* provides useful tools and techniques to drive accountability and a collective focus on results throughout your organization."
—Damon Gersh, President and CEO, Maxons Restorations Inc.

THE
DISCIPLINED
LEADER

THE
DISCIPLINED
LEADER

Keeping the Focus on
What *Really* Matters

52

Concise, Powerful Lessons

JOHN MANNING

Edited by Katie Roberts

BK

Berrett–Koehler Publishers, Inc.
a BK Business book

Berrett-Koehler Publishers, Inc.
1333 Broadway, Suite 1000
Oakland, CA 94612-1921
Tel: (510) 817-2277 Fax: (510) 817-2278 www.bkconnection.com

Ordering Information
Quantity sales. Special discounts are available on quantity purchases by corporations, associations, and others. For details, contact the "Special Sales Department" at the Berrett-Koehler address above.
Individual sales. Berrett-Koehler publications are available through most bookstores. They can also be ordered directly from Berrett-Koehler: Tel: (800) 929-2929; Fax: (802) 864-7626; www.bkconnection.com
Orders for college textbook/course adoption use. Please contact Berrett-Koehler: Tel: (800) 929-2929; Fax: (802) 864-7626.
Orders by U.S. trade bookstores and wholesalers. Please contact Ingram Publisher Services, Tel: (800) 509-4887; Fax: (800) 838-1149; E-mail: customer.service@ ingrampublisherservices.com; or visit www.ingrampublisherservices.com/Ordering for details about electronic ordering.

Berrett-Koehler and the BK logo are registered trademarks of Berrett-Koehler Publishers, Inc.

Printed in the United States of America

Berrett-Koehler books are printed on long-lasting acid-free paper. When it is available, we choose paper that has been manufactured by environmentally responsible processes. These may include using trees grown in sustainable forests, incorporating recycled paper, minimizing chlorine in bleaching, or recycling the energy produced at the paper mill.

Library of Congress Cataloging-in-Publication Data

Manning, John, 1957-
The disciplined leader : keeping the focus on what really matters 52 concise : powerful lessons / John Manning ; edited by Katie Roberts. -- First Edition.
    pages cm
Includes bibliographical references and index.
ISBN 978-1-62656-325-4 (hardcover : alk. paper)
1. Leadership. I. Title.
HD57.7.M366 2015
658.4'092--dc23

                                2015003291

First Edition
20 19 18 17 16 15   10 9 8 7 6 5 4 3 2 1

Jacket Design: Kirk DouPonce, DogEared Design

To our MAP consultants
who help our clients become Disciplined Leaders
through purpose, truth, and wisdom.

Contents

Introduction

While there's no perfect leader, you've probably known some pretty good ones—and perhaps even a few who've been truly great. If I challenged you to describe what makes great leaders great in a few key words, what would come to your mind? As president of a general management consulting firm called Management Action Programs, Inc. (MAP), I asked our consultants this question, and the word *disciplined* came up repeatedly.

In doing research for this book, however, I was curious to find out if people knew what a Disciplined Leader was. So I started asking a lot of other people, and this informal research project turned out to be quite an eye-opening exercise. The majority of people couldn't give me a clear answer. Many could readily cite examples of the greatest, most famous leaders. Some rattled off leadership traits, describing their favorite leader's style, as well as a few derogatory trademarks of their not-so-favorite leaders. A few quickly went off on a tangent, talking about the dire need for great leadership, not only in business but in our world. However, in spite of the varied feedback, every person I asked struggled with summarizing in one simple sentence what highly Disciplined Leaders always do to achieve significant results. It became clear this book could be a unique opportunity to define what a Disciplined Leader is and provide insight into becoming one.

But I also realized there was a problem. While the subject of The Disciplined Leader certainly piqued people's interest, not everyone I spoke with was immediately in love with the idea of The Disciplined Leader because they weren't sure what I meant by "disciplined." This was understandable. Different perceptions about the concept of discipline exist, and many of them are anything but uplifting. For some of us, the very word discipline may conjure up ideas of punishment, whether emotional or physical memories or a combination of both. For others, it might remind us of a very specific, rigid experience with learning, perhaps one that included old-fashioned educational rigor, hands getting slapped by a ruler, perfect penmanship, remaining in control at all costs, and ascribing to a sort of God-like admiration for the teacher and principal—or else! Discipline may trigger memories of a particular religion or even an oppressive government.

As societal attitudes and norms associated with parenting, education, religion, government/politics, and lifestyles have changed over the past fifty or so years, the notion of discipline has evolved into something of a black sheep. For the purposes of this book, I want you to think of discipline in this more positive, supportive context: *discipline is the consistent application of certain mindsets and actions that are vital for your success.* It's closer to the Merriam-Webster definition, "an orderly or prescribed conduct or pattern of behavior," and it's rooted in a relentless commitment to "self-control" and great habits.

In business, the element of discipline is at the heart of an organization's success. That's a truism I noted in my professional experiences with Fortune 500 companies I worked with over thirty years, as well as something I've found in working with MAP throughout the past decade. Within these organizations, I've consistently witnessed how discipline, which must always start with a leader, accelerates the excellence of organizations.

That self-controlled, consistent adherence to certain mindsets and actions ultimately develops and drives the very best leaders and businesses.

However, because discipline is misunderstood or not as valued as it has been in even more recent decades, the United States—and some might argue the world—is experiencing a cultural leadership crisis. Simply talking about discipline in leadership just makes people anxious despite the alarming rate of business failure. Every month, more small businesses in the United States, defined as 500 or fewer employees, close than start up. Yet of those that make it beyond the first few years, half fold within five years while more than 70 percent fail within ten years, according to the Small Business Development Center and the U.S. Census Bureau.[1] And one need only pay attention to media headlines to learn leaders of large corporations are struggling, too. Big brands, including Yahoo, Groupon, and Sears, are just a few of many that have not hesitated to replace their top leaders to remain in the game. Clearly, there's a great demand for the kind of discipline I've defined, and, most importantly, there's a critical need for leaders who honor and adhere to that discipline.

At MAP, we define The Disciplined Leader as someone who consistently excels at using the right mindset and actions to achieve results. This is done by "Focusing on The Vital Few" and ignoring or delegating The Trivial Many—a model for leadership that's based on the Pareto Principle. The Pareto Principle is commonly known as the "80/20 Rule." In MAP's fifty-four years of experience, we've learned The Disciplined Leader is someone who focuses on the 20 percent of activities that drive 80 percent of results under three core areas of leadership:

1) Leading yourself
2) Leading your team
3) Leading your organization

Within each of these core areas of leadership, The Disciplined Leader learns to identify The Vital Few. These become the 20 percent of habits and actions that will drive 80 percent of the results tied to their most precious asset—*people.*

The best leaders I've known all demonstrated excellent leadership characteristics (e.g., trustworthy, courageous, good communicators, etc.), some of which were stronger than others, depending on each leader's unique talents and abilities. But here's what these leaders all did well: they consistently disciplined themselves to focus on what really matters—again, people. They knew it was their people who were the driving force behind their products and services, so they learned to leverage that. What's more, these Disciplined Leaders stood out because their habits and practices aligned to their belief. And that made them exceptional.

Today, while there are many leaders who know deep down they should value this asset above all others, they don't do it. That's because their activities don't align with this mindset. Consequently, their habits and practices often tell a very different story about what they value most.

Case in point: Since 1960, MAP has helped accelerate sustained growth and development for over 15,000 organizations and 170,000 business leaders nationwide. When our consultants begin working with our clients, they often ask these leaders, "What is your business's most important asset?" Right on cue, they usually respond, "Our people." Most everyone gets it— people are *the* vital asset.

Then our consultants dig deeper: "What percent of your budget do you allocate to develop your people?" Silent, the clients usually respond with a wide-eyed stare. Breaking the awkwardness of the moment, the consultant next asks, "Well, how much are you planning to spend on products or equipment?"

At this point, most executives immediately pipe up, stating a specific number or at least a close estimate. They easily recall how much money they've allocated for the new phone system, facilities, computers, copy machines—the tangible things of business.

Again, the consultant says, "OK, you've got that down, so what's your most important asset?"

And this time, they get it. The point is all too clear: either they have no clue what they're spending on the development of their people, or the number is so small compared to expenditures for other business assets that it's rather embarrassing to confess it.

However, they soon learn they are not alone in their error or oversight. These professionals are representative of the many business leaders who, for countless reasons, underinvest in their people and their own leadership development. More importantly, there is a silver lining: making the commitment to shift priorities, putting people first, is something they can accomplish through commitment and focus.

Understanding this is a major factor in the success of many of MAP's clients. It is also a cornerstone to the MAP Management System™, a proven management system that's grounded in engaging and aligning employees through discipline, accountability, and achievement.

As stated, The Disciplined Leader knows how to "Focus on the Vital Few" and ignore or delegate The Trivial Many. That's what I'm encouraging you to do so you, too, can become a Disciplined Leader, a model for leadership excellence. It may be tough, but call upon your willpower to stop, delegate, and ignore whatever is trivial and detracting from your ability to focus on your most critical asset—people.

How to Use This Book

Here in this book, you'll find fifty-two meaty tips to help you become The Disciplined Leader. The information is based on the collective wisdom of MAP's professional expertise and key client-consulting experiences. It is categorized into three parts, the core areas of leadership responsibility: leading yourself, leading your team, and leading your organization.

To get the most out of this book, read all the tips, using each part as a source to extract your "Top Three" Vital Few for each part. In other words, after you've read each of the three parts (or skimmed the chapter headlines and chosen a shorter number to read), pick out the top three lessons that resonate most for you—what you know is really important in terms of developing and sustaining your leadership, your team, and your organization. At the end of this process, you should have nine Vital Few selected. From that list, we're going to challenge you to prioritize those nine to determine the "Top Five" Vital Few. These five will be the ones you want to take immediate action on once you finish this book.

To help, we've provided a *Vital Few Template* at the end of the Introduction. It will give you a place where you can record your "Top Three" Vital Few for each part and "Top Five" Vital Few for the book. Once you've identified your "Top Five," flip to those chapters and revisit the suggested action steps in relationship to the lesson you have learned, the habit that should be adopted, or the mindset you must embrace. Record those action steps (or add your own) into the template.

If we were coaching our clients, talking about the Vital Few needed to become The Disciplined Leader, we could easily pull from the guidance and solid insights offered from within the pages of this book. Hopefully, you will find value here, too. Use this book as a guide to help you learn your Vital Few and build effective leadership strategies to support those vital aspects of your leadership. What's offered here is a decades-proven process to transform you into The Disciplined Leader, a solution that provides critical, clear focus on what really matters.

VITAL FEW TEMPLATE

Name:_____   Date:_____

1. Book Part #I Vital Few: **PART #I**
    - _____
    - _____
    - _____

2. Book Part #II Vital Few: **PART #II**
    - _____
    - _____
    - _____

3. Book Part #III Vital Few: **PART #III**
    - _____
    - _____
    - _____

"Top Five" Vital Few – Overall Book

1. _____

Action Steps	**When**	**ACTION STEPS**
    - _____   _____
    - _____   _____
    - _____   _____

2. _____

Action Steps	**When**	**ACTION STEPS**
    - _____   _____
    - _____   _____
    - _____   _____

(over)

Figure 1 *Vital Few Template*

7

3. _____

ACTION STEPS

Action Steps	When
• _____	_____
• _____	_____
• _____	_____

4. _____

ACTION STEPS

Action Steps	When
• _____	_____
• _____	_____
• _____	_____

5. _____

ACTION STEPS

Action Steps	When
• _____	_____
• _____	_____
• _____	_____

Figure 1 *Vital Few Template (continued)*

Part I

Where You Must Start

The Responsibility to Lead Yourself

The journey to becoming a Disciplined Leader, one whose understanding and focus on The Vital Few drives the success of its people, must start with you. Before you make strides to impact your team and organization, it's part of your leadership responsibility to hold up the mirror and peer honestly and deliberately at yourself, reflecting on how you've led others.

You do that by examining your values and beliefs. You assess your traits that enhance or deflect from your leadership capabilities, paying attention to what you've been good at and not so good at in the past. You also recognize what you really cherish and are passionate about in your career and outside of work. You gain understanding of how your personal and professional lives interconnect and serve one another, and what the balance between the two look like at the end of the day.

Why go to all this effort? Because if you don't know these things about yourself and understand how they impact your ability to lead effectively, it will be impossible to understand how to make the right changes in your leadership—the ones that inspire you, your team, and the organization as a whole to act and deliver results.

Some years back, I was managing a business unit with three hundred employees (including fifteen managers), working seventy-hour weeks, and overlooking the importance of caring for myself. I started skipping healthcare check-ups and missing routine appointments. I wasn't eating healthy and failed to exercise and get adequate sleep. All these oversights and bad habits started creating stress and wreaking havoc on my personal and professional life. I found myself exhausted and run down physically, emotionally, and mentally. Then, after a few back-to-back wake-up calls, I suddenly realized a powerful truth: If I wanted to succeed in both my personal and professional life, I had no choice but to change my ways. So I did, and it has made all the difference.

Now perhaps you're thinking this is just pure common sense. But how many of us have had times when we've put the business ahead of ourselves? Not caring for our self—ignoring the importance of health, fitness, and wellbeing—is indicative of that classic personal-professional imbalance.

At MAP, we see this happening with leaders all the time—it's one of the most common reasons why company executives and managers suffer emotionally, mentally, and physically. The fallout then hurts everyone and everything in these leaders' paths.

But addressing this and other leadership "sins" of the self is easier said than done. It requires acute personal discipline, a fervent willingness to change, the ability to implement corrective action, and the relentless commitment to adopt new mindsets and habits.

Here, in this part, you'll find a collection of nineteen hearty tips that can stand alone and support you in your job to lead yourself. You're free to cherry-pick and read the ones that stand out to you initially if you wish. But if you can, read them all—start to finish, beginning to end. They are presented in a logical, sequential order, a sort of natural path of inspiration, empowerment, exploration, challenge, and insight that aligns with practical, commonsense coaching. But you'll find that they all demand your attention because developing your own personal leadership is the bedrock upon which your other two leadership responsibilities are built. Your personal leadership competency is the base of everything else you do to lead your team and organization.

As outlined in the introduction, this book provides a process for helping you identify your Vital Few. So when you read through these tips, highlight those subjects that trigger emotion, spark a fire, or simply stand out because your gut is telling you it's time to work on them. Perhaps identify ten or fewer because at the end of the part, you'll then choose your "Top Three" Vital Few—those mindsets and habits you will focus on to accelerate your ability to lead yourself.

Make the Commitment

Through life's lessons, you may have come to realize that when you are truly engaged in something, you naturally focus better and almost always achieve a greater outcome. You may have also noticed that your level of engagement for learning is significantly influenced by how you feel emotionally, mentally, and physically. When these aspects of you are in balance, you feel like you are on fire—nothing can stop you. Yet when things are misaligned, you're more prone to experience fear or failure, during which discord, imbalance, and even disease can rear their ugly heads and threaten to destroy the body-mind-spirit balance that's so critical to your well-being.

Change that results in personal growth and achievement is rewarding but rarely easy. For example, when I was very young, my mom enrolled me in swimming lessons at the local city center. To complete the class and be eligible for the next level of lessons, you had to swim the length of the entire pool without grabbing hold of the side. I failed miserably. In fact, I barely let go of the side of the pool during the whole ordeal and was one of just a few kids who didn't pass. Why? Even though I took the lessons and did the work every week, I wasn't ready for the big test, and it reminds me of other times in my life when I started something but didn't hit my goal or finish it. Whenever that has happened, I've examined the root cause of my failures and realized I was the culprit. I wasn't *ready* for the challenges.

But that's not the end of the story. My mom reenrolled me in the same class, and the second go-round was a different experience. Well before I took my first lesson, I made a personal commitment to pass the test come hell or high water. I would lie in bed and picture myself reaching the other end of the Olympic-size pool and see my mom's approving smile. I didn't know it at the time, but I was creating a vision of success. I took the class again, and on the big day of the test, I achieved success! Now I have to admit, I dog-paddled the whole way. (I was the youngest kid in my class!) But this solution worked, and I achieved my goal.

The need to get engaged and make a commitment to change is something our clients must accept, particularly when beginning the process of improving their personal leadership. For example, we had a client at MAP who was the owner of a chain of family-style restaurants. He thought he could turn around his business by using only a few parts of the MAP program. But when he attended MAP's 2.5 day executive workshop, he realized the degree of change required, and only then did he fully commit to the right mindset and embrace the emotionally, physically, and mentally challenging work. Doing so became the catalyst to his successful leadership and business transformation.

I am confident that you have many similar stories about getting in the right mindset to make change happen. Making the commitment to learn something significant or new takes energy, focus, and determination. When you are not mentally ready to make changes, you find ways to resist them.

To get results, be fully present and get involved with this book's journey. In doing so, you will maximize the benefits of your time and effort. As you move through the lessons offered here, check in with yourself and continually assess whether or not you are present and committed. If you're not, take action to correct the imbalance.

Here are some ways to stay on track:

Be mentally engaged. To make positive change, you've got to get in a positive mindset. Have you ever noticed that when you put your mind to some challenge, you can usually succeed? It's not an accident because success starts with the belief that you can reach your goal. Most leaders want to do a good job and want to be great at their responsibility to lead themselves—just like you. When you mentally commit and create focus, you can get it done. Adopt an "it's time to change" mindset, pushing out thoughts that will distract or deter you.

Be physically engaged. When you're feeling good physically, you have the ability to concentrate more and be more productive. If you want to maximize your leadership potential, it's critical to take care of your health and well-being. A regular routine for eating healthy meals, getting enough sleep, and exercising will help sustain a state of physical readiness.

Be emotionally engaged. Disciplined Leaders realize that they can't control everything happening around them but are conscientious about how they react and consistently choose the "higher ground." A perfect example of this was when George W. Bush received the 9/11 news while meeting in front of an elementary class in Florida. Realizing that he needed to maintain composure in front of these school children, who had no clue what the president had just learned, he generally appeared calm and let the children finish their presentation. Yet he obviously had the weight of the world on his shoulders. Bush and so many other leaders have been in countless situations in which they've disciplined themselves to maintain control over their emotional reactions.

You, too, have the ability to be in complete command of how you handle whatever is thrown your way. There are many things in life you can't control, so you must develop the ability to maturely manage your emotions. Of course, if you're physically and mentally alert, it will help with your emotional engagement as well. All of these elements tie together when we're talking about creating that state of engagement from which you can launch, commit to, and excel in leadership.

In Summary: The Disciplined Leader takes charge first with an inward focus. To become fully disciplined, balance and sustain your state of readiness on a physical and emotional level. Equip yourself with the physical energy and mental focus to optimize the disciplines put forth in this book. Be disciplined enough to overcome the fear of what those disciplines are—keep reading.

Take Action!

✓ Conduct a self-analysis of your life balance and identify areas that need focus and commitment. Consider all aspects: physical, knowledge, stress, life/work balance, and temperament under fire.

✓ Create accountability for improvement based upon your self-analysis. Develop a written plan to address what needs work and add deadlines for each activity in the plan.

✓ Start a daily journal to create focus and monitor progress on your plan.

Exercise Courage

The word *courage* takes its roots in the Latin word *cor*, which means the "heart." It should be no surprise that calling upon your courage to overcome whatever challenges you must face, whether in your personal life or leadership journey, will require heart, steadfast bravery, and sheer guts—and not just on occasion. Depending on the habit you're trying to break, the practice you're aiming to implement, or the change you're trying to drive within yourself, invoking your courage may become a regular, even daily practice for you.

Without courage, you may struggle to remain focused on The Vital Few. You will struggle to overcome difficult challenges. Courage is a requirement for facing your fears, doing things differently, and applying any new habits that align with and support your goals.

That said, fear is a natural emotion—we all have it to some degree or another. In fact, many MAP clients struggle with fears of failing. What we help them understand is that having no failures is evidence that someone is too cautious and not taking enough healthy risks in business. But as you'll come to find,

17

great leadership isn't just about facing fears but taking positive action *in spite of* your fears. As you experience success, your confidence will grow, and those fears simply won't be so frightful anymore.

Here are a few ways to find your courage:

Look the fear in its face. There's nothing magical about how to conquer what's causing your anxiety. The best way is to stand up to it, look at it, and take it head on. For example, after one of MAP's 2.5 day executive workshops, one attendee had a clear realization about the seriousness of the problem she had. In a follow-up meeting, this CEO confided to her MAP consultant that she had a fear of presenting to her board of directors. She had a bona fide phobia of public speaking. It was particularly elevated in stressful situations, such as during monthly meetings in which she had to provide company performance updates. The board members sometimes asked tough questions, and she didn't always have answers—something that made her feel insecure and weak. Through coaching, she discovered how big a barrier her fear was. She also came to understand how important it was to face her fear around public speaking and feeling she always needed to have the right answer. Simply acknowledging the fear was a big step. But the even bigger step was her decision to discipline herself to act against it. It was also her only option if she ever hoped to mitigate, if not eliminate, her fear altogether.

Create a plan of attack. Sometimes working a fear over and over in your mind can make it feel larger than life. That's what happened with this particular CEO— the more she thought about presenting in front of her board of directors, the bigger her fear grew. After deciding to face it, she worked with her MAP consultant on how she would fight it. She built a plan and implemented a process for managing public-speaking situations with greater calm and ease. She received training in public speaking, learned tools and tricks to help her improve, and invested more time into planning for her presentations. Most important, however, she learned and embraced a very freeing and important truth: to admit you do not always have the answers is more a sign of strength than weakness. So in dry runs with her MAP coach, this CEO learned to confidently say, "I don't have the answer, but I am willing to get back to you in 'x' amount of time." In essence, she took action against what she feared specifically by using a plan that gave her direction and a way to deal with it. This solution washed away a lot of worry. Speaking to the board of directors became something she could confidently manage.

Acknowledge when you succeed. Like this CEO who, despite her fears, had a lot of talent and accomplishments, you have probably done a lot more right than you've done wrong in life. You may be in the habit of taking such past success and accomplishments for granted—but don't. Part of sustaining your confidence is choosing to think more about your successes and less about your failures. Therefore, think about your personal success stories, the goals you have achieved, or anything else you've mastered. Scrutinize how your actions played a role in these big wins. This understanding can empower you to feel more confident and capable in general. Use this perspective to confirm, inspire, and grow your courage. Only you can cultivate and harvest your own courage, a required resource for your job as a leader.

In Summary: No one is without fears. The Disciplined Leader manages fears by first acknowledging them, analyzing them, and dissecting them. Doing what you fear will minimize the power fear has over you, boost confidence, and enable you to move beyond it. Create a plan to face your fears, one by one, and celebrate successes along the way, one by one.

Take Action!

✓ Make a list of your fears—what personal activities and work demands cause you the highest level of anxiety or surface insecurities?

✓ Establish accountability by writing a specific plan of action for each fear or habit you identified.

✓ Look for a role model, such as a well-known leader or someone with whom you work, who has good habits around those issues you've identified. Observe what that individual is doing differently. If possible, ask for guidance from that person.

Manage Your Worries

In your efforts to build greater courage, you might find yourself preoccupied with worry. The origins of the word *worry* are in the root words for choke or strangle. Worry is a toxic emotional condition that can feel like it's choking us at times, even though most of what we worry about doesn't ever happen. Nevertheless, many of us spend a lot of energy on the "what ifs" in life. We often find ourselves thinking about threats, pitfalls, and failures—a mindset that, like fear, can easily spiral out of control and hold you back from reaching your potential.

It's important for you to spot worry and realize its symptoms. Anxiety and procrastination can paralyze your potential to lead effectively. Chronic worrying can not only keep you from acting when you need to the most, but it can also blow you off an already windy course, prevent goal achievement, and crush dreams. Worse, it may even fuel compulsive and self-defeating behaviors.

MAP had a client whose vice president of human resources was struggling with her boss, the CEO. Specifically, the CEO wasn't listening to all the recommendations that the VP was making to support the management team. Therefore, the VP was both frustrated and worried. In the end, however, the VP couldn't control her boss, only her worries. So MAP coached her to invest more energy into those areas and aspects of her work that she could control. The result was reduced stress and anxiety.

We all struggle with worry. Try to make a new personal commitment to courageously ignore what's out of your hands, zero in on the present, and then act on what you can control.

Here are a few suggestions to help you leave your worries in the wind:

Understand that worrying is *not* a solution. Some people get stuck in a worry rut, where they seemingly enjoy or feel comfortable dwelling in their anxiety. There are also those who believe that by constantly thinking about what could happen, they're going to be prepared for whatever comes their way. They allow worrying to be the strategy for managing fears about the future. Most of their anxieties are about things that won't ever happen. Worse, they spend a lot of time fretting over what eventually amounts to a lot of nothing. What's the lesson for you? Anything that needlessly robs you of your time, energy, and other precious resources is destructive to you and your leadership. Remember: the Vital Few, not the Trivial Many.

Surface your worries. One of the best ways to address worries effectively is to get them out of your head by talking with a trusted confidant, someone who can help you sort through your thoughts, feelings, and options. It could be a mentor—a coach who can provide much--needed perspective and help you achieve greater clarity and calm. If you'd prefer not to talk to someone, simply writing down your worries on paper can be useful. Carve out a few minutes every week or day (if necessary) to make a list of those troubles. Categorize your list: (1) what you can control; and (2) what you cannot control.

Reduce worries. Once you identify what you can control, create an action plan. For example, if you're worried about losing your job but see that event as something you can likely prevent, then ask what steps you can take to do just that. Perhaps you will work more hours, show more enthusiasm at work, nurture key relationships, learn new skills, and so on. There are no guarantees in life, but if you proactively take control where you can, you'll most likely reduce your worries.

In Summary: As with fears, The Disciplined Leader gets a grip on useless worries that can spiral out of control. To lead others, your first responsibility is to lead yourself. Doing so requires controlling and combating worries. Failure to manage anxieties will adversely influence your ability to lead.

Take Action!

✔ Make a list of things you can control—and those you can't control. Develop an action plan to tackle what's controllable and prioritize your list. Periodically review this list and update it.

✔ Gather a close group of friends and/or colleagues who can give you suggestions and advice on the things you worry most about. Give them the space to be honest with you.

✔ Read books and find other resources to help develop your problem-solving skills. You will diminish your worries as you become more adept at problem solving.

Know Yourself

Truly knowing yourself is a powerful lever for initiating personal growth and development. Over the years, many of the best business leaders I've worked alongside have always had an excellent sense of themselves—this was a common trait they've all shared. They knew their strengths and weaknesses, knew what they were passionate about pursuing personally and professionally, and lived their values.

It's been said there are several levels of knowledge. Knowing something for certain is the first. The second is thinking you know something. The third is knowing with certainty you do not know something. The fourth is the killer: not knowing that you don't know something. This last state of knowledge is the most dangerous. What do you not know about yourself that, perhaps, others know all too well?

Some time ago, at one of MAP's executive workshops, a client learned through his 360-degree feedback that he had a definitive problem with conflict avoidance. He'd hired a couple of friends to work with him, but these friends were now ruining his business and their friendship. Everyone in the company, except the leader, could see that he was afraid to stand up to these co-worker "buddies." However, once he got to the heart of the feedback and learned that he had a serious aversion to conflict, he went back to his company and changed his ways. Aware of his weakness, he took corrective action to strengthen it and evolved into a highly capable, much more respected leader.

How does this relate to your ability to lead yourself? When you know yourself well, you are better able to maximize your leadership potential. You will realize what's working for you and what's not. You will gain clarity on how to leverage your strengths and overcome your weaknesses. For example, you may fully realize that you need to drop some old habits that have gotten in the way of your success. At the same time, you will likely find it's time to take on some new, consistent practices to help you meet goals.

Change is hard. Just look at the millions of people in the United States who are struggling to change habits around diet and exercise but regularly fail at their efforts. A 2010 study conducted by researchers from the Penn State College of Medicine[2] showed that of the two-thirds of American people who are overweight or obese, only one in six had actually maintained the weight loss. This example shows how people commonly struggle with changes, and the reasons for their failures are many. Likewise, there are countless external reasons why making critical changes of all kinds is hard for us. However, most of our barriers to change rise from within.

We are creatures of habit, generally resisting what's different or new whenever we can in our personal or professional lives. Staying the same feels simply easier, causes less stress, doesn't disrupt our busy lives, and allows us to simply "be." But we all know resistance to change causes problems, particularly for leaders. Start by realizing that change isn't easy, but it is necessary for leadership growth and development. Anticipate that you'll hit some occasional speed bumps, perhaps even major setbacks, along the way. That's normal—don't let it surprise you.

As you adopt more of the right leadership habits, remember that change is a process, not an event. Part of initiating that process is an examination of the self, an analysis that can provide the building blocks upon which you can create your overall plan for improvement. As outlined below, it includes understanding your past, studying your present situation, and thinking about where you want to be in the future:

Study the past. Thinking about your past successes and failures is a good place to start. It provides transparency on what's happened and positions you for change. For example, has anyone ever said, "You know, you've had the habit of doing or saying X every time Y has happened?" This looking back is a powerful exercise for understanding what you've done to succeed. For example, maybe you've been a great communicator, a real star at persuading others to adopt your point of view. You've repeatedly used this skill in the past to sell your ideas and create excitement in others. Since good communication is vital to effective leadership, you should leverage this newly identified strength to make progress toward your goals.

On the flip side, you might uncover specific behaviors or habits that have gotten in the way of past goal achievement. Perhaps you might discover that, as the familiar definition of insanity states, you've been doing the same thing over and over again, always expecting different results. Looking back—spotting pitfalls in behaviors and actions and noting patterns of self-defeat—gives you a chance to dig deep and be honest about what you've done to trip up time and time again. That precious self-realization, the ownership of your own role in any past transgressions, is vital. It will inspire the mindset you'll need to finally quit bad habits for good.

Examine the present. If you want to make a lasting, personal change that results in any sort of sustained growth, you've got to take a hard look at your current situation. Conduct a situation analysis to identify what you're good at and what you are doing right.

Think about your job and explore what's been going well and why. Then shift your thoughts to determine where you're falling short of your potential. Identify the choices you're making that don't align with your career goals. How well are you managing your priorities? What obstacles are getting in your way? Developing an accurate snapshot of your current situation will better equip you to create a vision for your future.

Imagine the future. The first step in imagining the future is to gain clarity about who you want to be and what you want to accomplish. Do you want to be a better boss, someone who is highly respected? Perhaps you're dreaming of landing a job that will take you to the next level as a leader. Or maybe you're wishing to score your very first opportunity to lead people, a situation that will become a solid springboard for future opportunities. Once you have a good grasp on what success looks like for you, picture yourself as that successful you in the future. This would be the future version of you, who *has* accomplished your goals, feels in control of life, and has found personal and professional fulfillment. How would that make you feel? In your vision, you hopefully have feelings of joy, confidence, and satisfaction. Use the vision to unlock inspiration and provide direction for your leadership path.

In Summary: Truly knowing yourself is a foundation for positive change. The Disciplined Leader knows studying the past and present, especially with the frank cooperation of friends and colleagues, yields excellent insight into personal strengths and weaknesses. Creating a future vision of yourself—call that a long-term goal—will fuel personal transformation and growth.

Take Action!

✓ Make a list of your "Top Five" professional accomplishments and skills. For example, what have you done in the past that you're proud about listing on your resume?

✓ Creat a list of present habits and actions and identify those that require change. Develop a plan to make those changes and overcome your obstacles.

✓ Identify five changes in routines you could do tomorrow that are easy, regardless of how mundane they are, such as taking a different route to work just for the heck of it.

Be Truthful

This book would not be complete without a lesson on truthfulness. Telling the truth is more than just a key aspect to good leadership. It is the best way to live your life. Our level of integrity defines who we are at our core. Truthfulness is the golden thread that binds good lives, good relationships, and our very legacy. Over the course of my career, I have conducted hundreds of job interviews, and most candidates tell me one of their values is integrity. Why? Because being an honest person who speaks and acts truthfully is so integral to living a good life, maintaining wonderful relationships, and establishing that great legacy.

The Disciplined Leader consistently tells the truth. Of course, being truthful is always easier when you are talking about the good stuff at work. Obviously, it's much more challenging when you're talking about what's gone wrong or giving bad news. The longer I live and participate in the business world, the more I realize telling the truth is almost always the correct choice, painful or not. There are ways to communicate with tact; a harsh reality can be delivered in a constructive way.

Why, then, do some leaders sugarcoat or downright lie about the state of business or how their employees are performing? Fear. And sometimes ignorance. They're afraid they're going to come across as weak, and they often simply don't understand or know how to "speak the truth" to staff or employees.

At times, you may also feel conflicted about delivering honest, albeit challenging communications with those you manage. But put yourself in your employees' shoes. They can't achieve their goals unless they have an idea of how they're truly performing and how they can take corrective action to improve their performance. So whether you're being honest about individual performance or the company's health, letting people know where they stand and being frank about the facts is the best approach. The truth will set the stage for a candid workplace culture, which is a pillar to an accountable, productive workforce.

Assess your overall life with truthfulness as the standard. Do you consistently tell the truth to your family, friends, and co-workers even if it is uncomfortable or unpopular? If you uncover areas where you need to make improvement, make a commitment to the needed changes. These changes will align with your desire to become a truly great leader who inspires others to grow and succeed.

Here are three applications for being truthful:

Be honest with yourself. As you contemplate the future you that you're exploring through this part of the book, don't leave truthfulness behind. It's your foundation, who you truly are, and a way for detecting what you need to change. If you can't take an honest look at yourself and who you are today, you won't be able to move forward. You need that benchmark or reference point for setting goals, measuring progress, and creating accountability. If you're not truthful with yourself, you'll most likely be incapable of being honest with others. This inability to be truthful impacts so many aspects in life, making it less fruitful.

Make truthfulness your mantra. We all struggle with the truth at times. Bend the truth in your mind, and it becomes impossible to be candid with yourself, other people, and all the situations you face in your environment. However, when you make truthfulness your mantra, it's much easier to be honest about whatever comes your way. When you have those tough calls to make or need to communicate something important, stay grounded in truth.

Use truth to act fast. In essence, truthfulness is a change accelerator—one that always starts with you. Operating from that space within, you can then make decisions and choices that will reflect your inner wisdom, self-discipline, and integrity. You'll also become equally empowered to prohibit negative self-talk that might rationalize your thoughts away from cold, hard truths. You'll be able to spot and stop the habit of making excuses, particularly the kind that have tried to knock you off the path of integrity.

In Summary: The Disciplined Leader makes integrity a guiding principle to define his or her leadership and build its legacy. Truthfulness is one of the most important virtues of human behavior. Understand that the truth itself cannot hurt you; it is what you do with the truth that can do harm if handled badly.

Take Action!

✓ Make sure your core values include something around integrity or truth.

✓ Recognize situations or people where you struggle to be candid. Recognize internal inhibitors that undermine your truthful ways, including rationalizing, making excuses, and pushing blame.

✓ Practice the principle of communicating with candor in all personal and professional relationships.

Have Humility

People love a leader who is confident, but they don't like leaders who are arrogant. That's sometimes a hard message to get across to both rising and veteran leaders alike, considering how the media and society often praise and promote celebrities, politicians, and other people who act high-and-mighty. However, there's really no bigger turnoff than an arrogant leader who behaves entitled or consistently communicates to others that their ideas and opinions don't matter. Like we said earlier, it isn't always right to be right.

As someone who is striving to lead effectively, you want to watch out for arrogance. Make a commitment to become conscientious about managing this behavior and balance your ever-growing confidence with steadfast humility. Listen to and value people's points of view. You'll learn more from others and naturally attract people, build stronger relationships with them, and earn their respect.

Over the years, MAP has worked with a number of exceptionally talented clients in all the major industries. When we first started working with some of these clients, they were arrogant. The notion they might not know all the answers to their problems was inconceivable to them. Moreover, when they first came to MAP, they were struggling to get the results they wanted from their organizations. Yet they never thought their egos might be a big part of what was in the way. These types of leaders have traditionally been tougher to coach. But some who stuck with the coaching managed to double and triple profits and revenues. What was the common thread in their eventual success? These leaders came to admit they did not have all the answers. They were able to let go of the ego and ask for and accept help.

Regardless of the industry, some leaders still sometimes succeed in life despite this toxic characteristic. It's daunting, really. But are they truly successful if they've hurt others in their leadership journey or if they left a damaged reputation in their wake? The lesson here is, you are responsible for how you carry and lead yourself.

How do you know if you've got some issues about being arrogant? Think about leaders you've known who've demonstrated this quality, note their behaviors, and ask yourself if you're exhibiting the same ones. Essentially, arrogance translates into someone who is all about themselves or who:

- doesn't invite, listen to, and value others' ideas and opinions;

- thinks and regularly communicates that her/his way is always the best or only way;

- uses lots of "me" and "I" versus "you" and "we" language;

- acts entitled, such as always going first or deserving the best;

- makes overbearing, presumptuous decisions or statements;

- takes an anti-teamwork approach;

- seems to have a lot of unexplained enemies;

- imposes her/his will on others; and

- provides lots of unsolicited, unwanted "advice."

It's not necessarily easy to swap out arrogance for confidence. If you need to change, realize it's going to require hard work to achieve a style of leadership that is confident yet retains an air of humility, asks more for input, listens better to others, and takes time out to engage co-workers or direct reports, those you manage directly. These are all very doable disciplines that can produce transformative results for your leadership credibility and, eventually, earn that much-needed respect. Here are three habits to enhance humility:

Look beyond you for answers. Read and learn about some of the most famous leaders and note how arrogance has hurt some while the right dose of confidence has helped others. These are leaders who've learned how to strike the right balance in their behavior. For instance, if you read books about Gandhi, Nelson Mandela, or Dwight Eisenhower, you will learn that these impressive role models were great leaders who exuded the virtue of humility while remaining extraordinarily confident. You can also look toward people you know personally who, although they may have much to brag about, are very humble about what they have, what they've accomplished, and how they've achieved success. These are self-assured types who also make humility look easy. Observe what they do or don't do, picking up their habits that will best serve you.

Adopt a teamwork mindset. Disciplined Leaders live and die based on the performance of their team. You will find that many of the best business leaders talk about their team and keep them in the spotlight, not talking about themselves. These leaders understand their role is to help their team be successful and give them credit every time credit is due. Through these actions, such leaders earn that crucial respect, build loyalty, and consistently get their desired results. They know that by recognizing others' successes, refraining from talking about their own accomplishments, is a part of humble leadership. These actions are the opposite of being selfish or only thinking about their own success.

Grow awareness of your verbal and body language. It's important to understand all you say and do creates an image of your leadership brand. Make sure to invite people to consistently share their thoughts and be genuinely encouraged about what they might tell you. Don't be too quick about shutting down their ideas. Perhaps you have an annoying habit of smirking or rolling your eyes when someone is trying to talk. Maybe you don't look people in the eye. Whatever you're guilty of, make a commitment to drop these bad habits and consistently find ways to replace them with good habits that reflect humility. The humble attitude is a genuine mindset, communicating you're no more important than others on your team. Take it to heart, and others will perceive you as open and welcoming as opposed to closed and uninterested.

In Summary: The Disciplined Leader knows controlling the ego is essential to teamwork. Humility is a great virtue of leadership that sends the message your ego doesn't rule the roost. Humility is about putting more focus on others and less on yourself.

Take Action!

✓ Talk less, listen more. Be someone who can truly listen to others and value their opinions.

✓ Identify a role model who consistently practices humility and study his or her style and behavior.

✓ Develop your leadership style like a branded product. You want others to trust that brand and always lean toward it.

Zero in on
Your Values

It's not uncommon for me to ask people what their values are and then get delayed responses or blank stares in return. Most people understand they have values, but they just can't articulate them easily. Why? Unless they've been prompted in some professional training exercise, their values are likely to be floating around in their head. They just never took the time to define them by asking which values were most important. If they never really had a clear definition of what a value is, then they struggle with clarifying what their values are.

Yet everyone has values—including you. Values tend to be reflected in your behaviors. For example, when you attend a funeral and a eulogy is given to describe the deceased as a good husband, wife, or friend who went out of the way to help others, this is actually a reflection of that person's values. This example demonstrates how people lived their lives according to values.

Problems surface when leaders overlook the importance of recognizing and aligning their values in key decision making. In fact, one of MAP's most seasoned consultants estimates that 70 percent of newly hired CEOs are not successful in a new position because their values and, specifically, how they're leading and managing according to their values, don't align with the values of the company that hired them.

This issue cropped up with a highly technical company. The company provided specialized services to governments yet upheld values that reflected a somewhat relaxed, open, and forgiving environment. When the company hired a candidate with a military background as its new CEO, this individual was acutely focused on driving results but ran his vendors and staff in an overly regimented, authoritative way. It quickly became clear that, despite certain strengths, this CEO's values didn't align with the company's values. He ended up being a total mismatch for that culture and was let go about a year after being hired.

Values are a big part of your unique identity and leadership. These guideposts shape your decisions and actions, playing a major role in defining who you are and what you do. Values are important for greater self-understanding, which, as mentioned in our previous lesson, is part of the groundwork for becoming a Disciplined Leader.

They can also provide insight into what's best for you personally and professionally. For instance, your values can serve as a tool for making career choices, everything from whether you accept a job or promotion to how you decide to handle work conflicts.

Disciplined Leaders regularly reference their values in critical decision making and rely on them when they are stuck between "a rock and a hard place." They use them to establish specific direction and get confirmation about those choices they've made. Over time, the practice of consistently aligning values to decision making, particularly as they relate to certain behaviors and actions, builds leadership credibility and respect. If you understand and commit yourself to your values, you can increase your chances of achieving your most important goals in life—and your people will notice!

Whether you're determining your values for the first time or revisiting them for a status check, the following process can provide the clarity you need:

Start with a master list of values. You've got a general sense of what's important to you, so make a master list of those values, not worrying so much about how many you have. Below are some examples of values to help get your wheels turning.

Passion	Accountability	Teamwork
Integrity	Trust	Humility
Service	Courage	Respect
Achievement	Discipline	Growth
Health	Commitment	Compassion
Encouragement	Dependability	Ethical
Family	Happiness	Financial
Charity	Gratitude	Work Ethic
Honor	Individuality	Leadership
Loyalty	Motivation	Learning
Openness	Persuasiveness	Optimism
Perseverance	Pride	Professionalism
Reliability	Prosperity	Self-control
Significance	Selflessness	Success
Stability	Vision	Wealth
Empathy	Results-oriented	Competitive

Figure 2 *Sample Values Chart*

Identify your core values. Now that you've identified the values that resonate the most for you, it's time to whittle them down to just a few core ones—which is often a little harder for people to do. For the purpose of this exercise, define your core values as your "Top Five." One of the best ways to determine those five is to ask some value-based discovery questions. For example, what's most important to you and what do you want to be known for? When were you the most successful in life—and why? What need or wish was met? How were you fulfilled? If you find it extremely important to uphold your integrity at work or with any other aspect of your life, then perhaps integrity is one of your core values.

Let your values guide you. Now that you've identified your core values, you have guiding principles to make solid decisions and pursue meaningful direction in both your personal life and work. When you align your behaviors to your values, you will feel happier and more satisfied. You will have your most important priorities in order as you make choices, change, and grow. After you've documented your core values, consider sharing them with people you trust to see if they agree with your list. From these discussions, you might find you need to make changes to your list.

In Summary: The Disciplined Leader holds certain values supreme and knows those values nurture and shape personal leadership and an orderly life. Values are the navigational tools for making the right choices and sound decisions. When your behaviors align with your values, you will be more fulfilled, perhaps even happier.

Take Action!

✓ Go through the process of identifying your core values and then write them down.

✓ Assess how your current behaviors and actions align with your core values. Develop corrective actions if you're in misalignment with your core values.

✓ Use your core values to proactively and consistently help you make decisions.

Recognize Your Talents

You are unique. Think about it: There are over seven billion people on our planet, and not one of them is identical to you. Study up a bit on the science behind DNA, and you'll quickly learn just how different you are from others working alongside you. While understanding what makes you unique can give you a leadership edge, realizing what's *extraordinary* about you is even better—those unique traits that are particularly special to you. Consistently work to emphasize, develop, or leverage these abilities and you'll eventually carve out a clearer, greater leadership advantage.

I firmly believe that there's something extraordinary about everyone. If you want to change and grow, you need to believe this about yourself. When you figure out and trust in how you're extraordinary, this revelation can create not only real satisfaction but also joy—both of which are powerful and motivating. You can then use this knowledge as a tool for achieving your goals and vision as a leader.

Many people I have worked with over the years haven't always known what makes them extraordinary. Often they haven't felt unique in any particular way. But each one has had a special set of experiences and skills that made them stand apart from others.

That said, maybe you are reading this and struggling to think of what makes you different. Or, perhaps you can't even contemplate the fact that, yes, you are extraordinary. If so, here are several ways to get insight, so you can leverage that to develop your leadership potential:

Examine what you love to do. There are so many things that we do as part of our daily routine and out of obligation. Think about some of the activities that you really love doing in your professional or personal life. What especially motivates, moves, or excites you? For example, maybe you really like mentoring others and playing a part in their growth and development. When you're personally involved in this activity, it triggers your most positive emotions because you're truly making a difference in the world.

Once you uncover what you love to do, dig deep and determine what specific aspects of it lift your spirit and make you feel good. Perhaps you really enjoy helping others grow, and your love for mentoring is partly a reflection of that. Maybe when you're coaching others, you thrive on sharing lessons learned, particularly with others who benefit from your gift. Greater understanding will give you the ability to align future activities to your passions, resulting in even more satisfaction.

Determine your best skills. To figure this out, ask, what do you do better than most other people you know? Often through our internal conversations, we focus on the negative. So it's important to think about what skills you have that do make you effective and different. Maybe you've got exceptional people skills, are super analytical, or have strong work ethic. Your best skills are whatever you've *learned* to do really well in life. If you are unclear about your skill set, ask people you know and trust to give you feedback. Understanding with crystal clear clarity what you do well will contribute to what makes you unique. Use this information to uncover future opportunities that will tap your strengths, influence people, and get results. This is what Disciplined Leaders consistently do.

Know your true gifts. Gifts are different from skills. While skills are learned and mastered, your gifts are innate and thus cultivated like seeds. You were born with them. What have you always been good at doing even from the time that you were a child? If you were extremely verbal and chatty, perhaps you're a natural born communicator. If you were agile and strong, perhaps you are a natural-born athlete. Like your fingerprint, your unique gifts are so personal, given only to you in a certain pattern, imprinted in a particular way and tied to your authentic identity. If you fail to recognize and sufficiently use your gifts, you will probably feel like you're missing the mark in life. Things will just never feel quite right.

In Summary: The Disciplined Leader has identified the Inner Extraordinary that is the foundation of his or her leadership. It's all about tapping your skills, gifts, and passions and using those things to develop both personally and professionally. It's about maximizing your leadership potential, sharpening your personal edge, and staying true to the *real* you.

Take Action!

✓ Answer the following questions to get clarity around what you do best:

- What work activity would you do for free because you enjoy it?

- What must others work at that comes naturally for you?

- What do you do that garners other people's praise? What do they say you are really good at?

- What are you passionate about?

✓ Ask family, friends, and mentors for their observations. What do they see about you that makes you unique? Use the questions above if appropriate.

✓ Read past performance reviews or other feedback to look for common themes related to areas or ways in which you exceeded expectations.

Get Out of
Your Way

When people fail in their responsibility to lead themselves, it's usually not because of something external to them or their situation. It's due to the fact that *they* get in their own way. Ever hear of the expression, "He's his own worst enemy"?

Sure, there are many barriers that can block someone's path and potential, everything from lack of resources to poor support from the boss or organization. But when you really take a close look at what prevents people from excelling and achieving their dreams, it's usually due to their own mindsets and actions.

What are some of the common roadblocks? Over the years, MAP has seen clients shortchanging their own development for any number of reasons. For instance, one client had a habit of constantly using bad language both with his staff as well as when communicating in more public situations, such as at industry-wide conferences and speaking engagements. Despite his clear intelligence and status as a leader, people were put off by his abrasive communication style. It prevented his ability to gain sustained respect, build partnerships, and achieve what could have been even more monumental success. He was in his own way.

In another classic case, a company CEO in the health-care industry cared too much about her patients. How was that possible? Well, she cared so much about personally tending to her current patients that she couldn't let go and delegate this responsibility to others. Consequently, she had no time to focus on growing her business. Meanwhile, a large audience of potential patients remained just that—potential versus real, paying ones. She was in her own way.

At the root of these and many other common issues are fundamental barriers around poor self-esteem, inability, and lack of knowledge or understanding. If given the power, these core obstacles can become career stallers. Unchecked, their symptoms can manifest into ways that make it impossible to move forward and excel.

Fortunately, you can control many things in life. *You* are one of them. When it comes to your stuff or your baggage, it's your call whether these obstacles, anything you're allowing to get in your way, get to keep their power. You have the final say on whether they will prevent you from doing or getting what you want from your leadership—and your life. You are the master of your attitudes and the driver behind your habits. Considering that we all tend to get in our way at some point, here are some ways to note and nix the problem if, indeed, *you* are the problem:

> **Understand your barriers.** Sometimes people go through the motions of their job, operating in a sort of "darkness" in which it is impossible for them to see what's happening around them. They may sense some barriers in their midst, but they need a light to see what those problems are and how they're affecting themselves and others. That was the case for one of MAP's clients whose addiction to excessive smoking was driving her co-workers crazy. Despite the fact that this individual had considerable talent, she took smoke breaks all the time. MAP's consultant gave her this feedback and then asked her some tough "why" questions. A lot of tough

stuff emerged. She realized it was mainly her habit that was not popular with her team and it could affect her health. The willingness to receive feedback and the courage to dig deep and get clarity turned the light on. This allowed her to see what was really going on and gave her the information she sought—a hard truth she needed to know.

Acknowledge that it's up to you to change. After MAP's client realized her smoking habit was a real, sizeable barrier to success, she took ownership of the problem and recognized it was time to quit. Quitting would take courage. It would take discipline. But it was the only solution for creating better relationships with her people, raising morale, and boosting productivity. She realized two important truths: your behaviors and mindsets belong only to you, and it's your job to own them and change for the better.

If you don't know what your barriers are, it's impossible to figure out how to tear them down. So carve out the time to reflect on what's blocking your potential. If you struggle figuring it out, get feedback from others you trust. Also, explore possible triggers around identified barriers, those situations that initiate bad habits. Spotting these roadblocks and knowing what drives them will provide direction around how to tear them down.

Realize the power of *you*. You have the power to set yourself up for growth and development. In this example of MAP's client, it was liberating for her to realize one of her biggest problems was a habit tied directly and only to herself. Tough as it would be to quit, kicking the habit was something she could control. This understanding created a sense of freedom that empowered her. The insight gave her the motivation she needed to quit. In the end, she did quit, much to the delight of her co-workers, family, and friends.

A powerful aspect to your leadership growth will involve a process for identifying your barriers, taking ownership of them, and then knocking them down. Getting out of your own way is part of leading yourself. Success with this area of development will be determined by your willingness to own your problems, remain strong in the face of temptation, and make wise choices.

In Summary: The Disciplined Leader knows what an Achilles Heel is and how to keep it from getting the best of him or her. Likewise, many times, the biggest obstacle to growth and development is *you*. Realize that you have complete power to get out of your own way and remove those self-made and self-sustained barriers to positive change. But first, you must uncover them; they are hidden from you but likely in plain sight of those around you.

Take Action!

✓ Identify times in your past where you've played a role in building your own barriers that prevented you from moving forward to excel.

✓ Make a list of your top internal barriers to making changes—the behaviors that get in your way, such as losing focus, rationalizing, overreacting to criticism, and others.

✓ As part of your development plan, establish strategies to mitigate each barrier that you've identified.

Push beyond the Comfort Zone

Part of leading yourself is learning when to challenge yourself at strategic moments in your professional life. When I look back at my career, several big professional growth spurts were directly attributable to when I pushed my comfort zone. These were times in which I had little or no experience with a particular area or in a certain subject. I had to learn on the fly as I took on and mastered those new projects or responsibilities, a strategy that enabled me to really accelerate my career. That made me a big believer in the importance of periodically pushing your comfort zone. From a professional standpoint, tackling something new has the power to build your capacity for success and is a great discipline worth pursuing.

MAP once worked with a company that was managing two very different business models: (1) low-margin yet dynamic products that consistently got lots of publicity and attention; and (2) boring but high-margin products that garnered little enthusiasm from the company's leadership and its staff. As MAP's consultant was helping the company to identify its Vital

Few, everyone realized that as uncomfortable as it made them feel, the company drastically needed to change its resource allocation and start investing heavily in building the lucrative, albeit lackluster division of their business. They all thought it would be super to be "rich and famous" but also agreed that "famous" could—and would have to—wait. The real challenge for everyone was to let go of what was fun and felt comfortable while focusing and building upon this less-riveting yet sturdier business bedrock. In the end, the payoff was huge: just one year later, the company had experienced a seven-figure, bottom-line turnaround.

To push your comfort zone, how do you decide where to start? The structure of this book allows you to review the lessons and determine your Vital Few practices that really stretch your comfort zone and are critical to reaching your leadership potential. How will you know what those are? The vital ones will give you the biggest bang for your buck in self-development, progress, and personal reward. This could include taking on habits tied to areas in which you have very little experience. Or, it might be taking on a new commitment outside your company, something that broadens your experience and opens doors to new connections and professional possibilities. Once you identify what you want to do or learn, incorporate that into your leadership development plan, so it becomes a real target—a challenge you're committed to addressing. Then, hold yourself accountable to ensure it happens.

Here are some considerations tied to pushing your comfort zone:

View learning as an opportunity to grow confidence. Knowledge is power. The more you know, the more equipped you will be to effectively lead and manage over the course of your career. Not only will you feel more in control, but you'll also display more confidence because of the prior experience you've gained by challenging yourself. When it comes to embracing knowledge and what's new, people working in the technology industry provide a perfect example for us all. They must have powerful self-initiative and motivational drive, particularly by endlessly innovating to remain cutting edge in their line of work. They can't fall behind in their field. If they do, it can put their careers, reputations, livelihood, and even their self-esteem at risk.

Trust in the power of learning. Early in my career, I developed a reputation for being someone who was motivated to learn new things and take on difficult assignments. One of the big benefits of this approach was that management noticed I was proactive about my professional growth. They started seeing me as different from some of my peers. As new internal job opportunities opened up, I successfully climbed the corporate ladder.

Likewise, if you are willing to push your comfort zone and learn new things, people will probably recognize your efforts, too. It's a great way to set yourself apart from others and get ahead more quickly in your career. As people notice, the efforts you've made will pay off— perhaps you'll land that breakthrough client, someone who never gave you the time of day until you took that self-initiative to become smarter or more skilled at business development. On top of this, your newfound skills and expertise could earn you a better position within your current company or a more challenging, exciting opportunity outside it. Maybe it will pan out in the form of greater financial rewards, a payback that can be particularly satisfying if you've personally invested hard-earned dollars, time, or other resources into your self-improvement goal. The benefit might not seem obvious or be immediate, but it will eventually become clear.

A compelling story on trusting in the power of learning comes from the 2005 commencement speech[3] delivered to Stanford University graduates by the late Steve Jobs. In the speech, he explained how his seemingly random decision to take a calligraphy class later contributed to his success in computers. When he and his design team built the first Macintosh, they developed it with the beautiful typography that is now an everyday feature to all computers today. When he first signed up for that class, he was simply doing something he enjoyed. The full benefit of what he learned didn't become clear until about ten years later in his life—but it certainly did become clear.

Make it fun! If you make the conscientious choice to view your self-improvement—even the professional kind—in a lighthearted, positive way, you can actually enjoy whatever it is you've decided to learn. Approach the goal you've set with a positive, grateful attitude, and your perception about the goal and the journey will simply feel easier, less like work, and more like fun. View this commitment as something you *want* to do, not something you *have* to do, thinking of it in terms of exploring fresh horizons, creating new relationships, pushing exciting personal boundaries, and so forth. When you set a goal to learn something new, actively plan for a way to make the experience enjoyable.

Some years back, I worked at a Fortune 500 company and led a cross-functional team tasked with automating our customer-service system for frontline employees. In doing this, my team and I were way outside our comfort zone mainly because the project was so massive. We experienced a lot of ups and downs. However, throughout the course of the project and even at its most challenging moments, we found ways to make it fun. We would celebrate small wins by going out to different restaurants and recognizing individuals who were making a difference. We also developed a process to acknowledge people who demonstrated commitment to the project, and this became so popular the entire company ended up adopting the recognition process.

We rewarded people who contributed to the project's success in small ways by giving them candy and little gifts, and, to our surprise, people had more fun with the small rather than large incentives. Our approach provided a lot of great laughs (endorphins!) and camaraderie amid the trials and errors of creatively collaborating as a team on such a lofty goal.

There are many things in life that aren't necessarily fun but must be done. So if you're going to take on something new in your professional development, building up the fun factor will make it more attractive and certainly more doable, too.

In Summary: The Disciplined Leader recognizes pushing the comfort zone can become a fun challenge that makes professional and personal growth more rewarding. Challenging your comfort zone can accelerate and lead to new career opportunities, building your potential to achieve your leadership goals.

Take Action!

✓ Make a list of things that you want to learn that will push your comfort zone. Incorporate your top picks into your self-development plan.

✓ Take a class in a relevant field that will push you in new ways and sharpen your skills.

✓ Seek more responsibility in the areas you want to develop. These areas can be inside or outside of work.

Drop
Defensiveness

It's part of The Disciplined Leader's job to sit in the hot seat
at times. People will look to us for explanations and hold us
accountable for problems. So it's only normal for us to get a
little defensive now and then. But do you ever notice yourself
regularly overreacting or becoming hot tempered too often? If
so, it's time to cool off.

Habitually defensive behavior creates an atmosphere in
which people walk on eggshells and struggle to communicate—primarily with you. That's dangerous for your business's
well-being because it can stifle transparency, ideas, and productivity. So discipline yourself to let go of defenses and display
confident, noncombative leadership by realizing you are not
always right and by welcoming feedback from others. This leadership trait will build your credibility and foster effective, re-
spectful, and forward-thinking communication.

How do you know if you're too defensive? Unless you've
had someone say you've got a problem, you need to pay attention to your communication style. Early in my career, I could be
defensive at times. After deciding to address the issue, I realized

it was likely related to my confidence and maturity as a leader. I knew this behavior could eventually improve with experience, wisdom, and time. But I didn't have time on my side. I couldn't just wait around in the hopes of getting wiser about managing myself or others. I needed to be effective right away.

So I looked toward some of my leadership role models for guidance. I noted how managing defensive tendencies was really a proactive process. If I took charge of my emotions even in dicey situations, I could become better at keeping my cool and facilitating and improving communication all around, the latter of which has always played a role in building a healthy workplace culture. The key was to manage those emotions in real time, and that's what the best leaders consistently worked at and gracefully mastered.

It's common to see people get defensive around company acquisitions that go wrong. Often overly invested both emotionally and financially, such leaders can't see how touchy their situation is. One of our clients ignored the warnings of his MAP consultant about the dangers of a particular acquisition. After going ahead with it, this leader turned a blind eye when the acquisition started draining company resources. He appeared unfazed by the devastating turnover in talent until a call from the bank snapped him back into reality: "Liquidate now or you'll get a call from the law." Finally this CEO got the picture, dropped his defensives, and started taking tough but necessary corrective action.

Being defensive is a common challenge with many people who take on or grow into leadership positions. But Disciplined Leaders learn to regularly combat defensiveness and rise above the fray, and this becomes a turning point in their careers. It can pave the way for the successful implementation of the practices within this book and position you for explosive potential. Dropping your defenses unlocks the door to learning, change, and growth. If you struggle here, consider these important "to dos" that are proven to reel back reactive behavior:

Pay attention to that gut. If you're sensing that you're being unnecessarily or overly defensive, it's time for self-examination. Where is it coming from and why? Are you willing to change? Answer these and other such questions if you've got a gut feeling your behavior is overly reactive as well as if you notice others having trouble communicating honestly with you.

Ask for feedback. Collect input on your behavior by having a candid talk with your direct reports, colleagues, or team members at work. Use an anonymous 360-feedback instrument, especially if you've cultivated a culture in which people don't feel comfortable speaking up about your leadership style. You could also ask a mentor for his or her honest opinion and get help creating the right questions to ask.

Once you've got the feedback, embrace it. View this input as a gift—one that can help you and your company improve. Genuinely *thank* such people for sharing whatever they've courageously chosen to tell you.

Be open to bad news. When you get it, don't react. Get more facts first. Why? Facts are powerful. They transform your perspective, enabling you to take the right corrective action to address your issues. So launch that fact-finding mission, keeping in mind that even the worst news can become a valuable lesson learned that spins your compass in the right direction. Don't fight it, and certainly don't shoot the messenger. This reactive leadership style can be a career derailer. It's a sure sign that your emotions, instead of your rational brain, are driving your behaviors.

In Summary: The Disciplined Leader learns, often after some trial and error, that letting go of defensiveness builds credibility, opens lines of communication, and enhances business relationships. Listening rather than reacting may yield information vital to your success. Being defensive about how right you are should prompt this question: *Is it always right to be right?*

Take Action!

✓ Actively listen. When people give you feedback about yourself, ask for clarity and specifics so you can fully understand the information. When you feel attacked, gain more understanding instead of taking a defensive stance.

✓ Take an individual assessment that identifies your behavior style and how you react to feedback. Understanding how you're wired will help you better manage your reaction to feedback.

✓ Ask colleagues to recall specific incidents in which you chose defensiveness over listening that led to distractions and distrust among the staff.

Eliminate the "Victim" Mentality

We have all worked around people—perhaps even bosses and other types of leaders—who've spent the majority of the time complaining about their job and all other aspects of life. You can spot these classic "victim" types from a mile away. They're eternally angry, stressed, or mopey, often saying things like, "It's not my fault," "I can't ever do this or that," and "I don't know how my life got this way." These personalities are trapped in a cycle in which they can't see their contribution to any of their difficulties. They drain positive energy out of the workplace because they're always having some variation of a bad day. Moreover, positive people have to go out of their way to maneuver around these personalities because the negative energy can be so downright toxic.

If you want to be a well-respected leader, you can't afford to act or think like a victim. This mindset and its associated behaviors are counter to the mindset and behaviors of strong, effective leaders. Also, good leaders attract people to them, while victims repel people away through the things that they believe, think, say, and do.

Some years ago, one of MAP's construction industry clients was really struggling with a manager who was overseeing business for him in a major city. The manager had that classic "poor me" attitude when asked about missed goals and his failure to secure new bids. Finally, enough was enough. The CEO told this manager that *he* was the root of the problem and so it was *he* who needed to solve it—or else! As a result, the manager took action against his victim-like mentality, hired a sales director, and immediately started getting more work for the company.

It is a certainty we will all face difficult times and become victims of circumstance in some way or another. You just can't escape it. But when you notice yourself in such situations, you can choose not to get caught in any eternal victimhood. You do this by controlling your attitude and how you consistently approach challenges big and small. Calling upon your strength and courage, you can fortify positive measures of self-discipline that will help you overcome obstacles and remain free from the grip of this vice. Here are some ideas how:

Retrain your brain. It's okay to feel sorry for yourself once in a while. But it is more important to get power over your thoughts, swapping out negative feelings that don't serve a good purpose with new, helpful ones that do. So if you find yourself thinking or speaking some version of, "It's not my fault, I couldn't help it," note it. But then ask, "What can I do to control my situation?" or "In spite of how I feel, how can I act to get closer to my goal?" If you can get into a habit of recognizing and replacing those negative internal and external conversations with positive, productive ones, you will have a more fulfilling outlook on life and work and also attract people who will follow your lead.

Don't get trapped. It is important to empathize with others who might be struggling at work or in their personal life. But you need to recognize when someone chronically chooses to play the role of victim.

Watch out! You could get sucked into their complaining. Avoid taking on that individual's mindset and self-defeating behaviors that will negatively affect you. It's very likely you will sometimes have to deal with people like this in life and at work, perhaps listening to their problems or frustrations. But then make a mental commitment not to let their troublesome ways trap you or stifle your potential.

Replace helplessness with hope. There is a bit of "victim" ingrained in us all. To some degree or another, everyone struggles with feelings of helplessness at times. Fortunately we have choices about how to manage our emotions in such situations. As a leader, the emotions you choose to own and exhibit really need to be those that collectively reflect a strong spirit of hope no matter the difficulty of the situation and regardless of whether you truly are a victim of circumstance or not. Because the workplace culture often has a way of taking on the personality of its strongest leader, be aware that through consistent strength and optimistic, powerful messaging, you won't just better yourself but will effectively impact others for the better, too. When people around you feel your optimism, they will also be encouraged to ward off thinking or behaving as victims.

In Summary: The Disciplined Leader knows how to attract followers through positive attitudes and beliefs. Being a victim repels people away through the things you believe, think, say, and do. Avoid playing the victim; display an optimistic leadership style.

Take Action!

✓ Jot down on paper some instances in which you felt like a victim. What resulted? How could you have handled those instances differently?

✓ Write down and memorize your philosophy for combating the victim mentality.

✓ Limit exposure to people and conversations that might suck you into that victim mentality.

See Mistakes as Opportunities

Let's face it: Everyone fails and falls short at times. We've all made mistakes, some of which could have been avoided. Yet how often do we add fuel to the fire by becoming our own worst enemies, overly criticizing ourselves for past transgressions? If you're like many leaders who tend to excel in life and work, you may find yourself being too self-critical of your mistakes or those innate flaws over which you have very little control. As was mentioned earlier, not having at least one failure may indicate you are overly risk-averse and not taking the occasional educated guess that could yield a big reward.

While taking responsibility for your actions and shortcomings is a healthy practice, dwelling on what's not perfect about you or what you've done wrong is ultimately unproductive. It can hold you back as you try to make progress through these lessons, stifle your self-esteem, and keep you stuck in countless other ways.

So instead of lying awake, stewing all night about how you've blown something in life or at work, flip that train of thought and develop a more productive, forward-thinking mindset.

Practice viewing your mistakes as opportunities to learn and improve. See each mistake as a catalyst for change. Look for the lesson learned, thinking how you can apply any takeaways to transform your life for the better.

For example, it's not every day that you hear a business leader tell her people, "Congratulations team—we made a big mistake—and everyone needs to celebrate it!" However, that's exactly what a MAP client said to her staff after a proposal mistake resulted in their losing a major business contract. Instead of getting down in the dumps, this leader pushed everyone to start exploring other opportunities and, specifically, more appropriate avenues for growth. Then, not long after losing that contract, the company learned the market it would have invested in essentially dried up and died. The lost contract ended up being not just a lesson learned in smart prospecting and proposal writing but a blessing in disguise—all of which was certainly worth celebrating.

Of course, cutting yourself some slack is sometimes easier said than done. It takes willingness, self-discipline, and self-control to let go of past transgressions. It also requires the ability to forgive yourself for mistakes and release self-limiting beliefs. You can grow and achieve despite past errors and innate flaws that are simply part of who you are. Knowing this will support you in your job: the responsibility to lead yourself.

Here are some strategies to help implement and strengthen this practice:

Stop replaying the scene. After making a mistake or doing something wrong, we often replay the scene in our minds, fretting over how we could have done things differently. While processing the event is healthy, tormenting yourself over it is not. It creates superfluous stress that can undermine mental and physical health. So always try to notice when the mind's movie projector starts rolling. Find a positive distraction—quick! Shift your thoughts elsewhere: Go exercise, meditate, deep breathe, call a friend—do something to stop vicious, cyclical thinking.

"Confessing" to a confidant or a mentor can also stop this mind trap. If you've made a mistake or failed in some way, discussing it with an unbiased confidant or mentor may release guilt, anger, or other detrimental feelings. Not only can sharing your humanity with another make problems easier to bear, but it can also open doors to fresh feedback, insights, solace, and even solutions.

Practice self-forgiveness. Whether you pray, meditate, or do some other activity to deal with mistakes, taking some sort of action is vital for self-forgiveness. Then as pointed out by author, public speaker, and physician Deepak Chopra,[4] "Even if you have no religious faith at all, the key to forgiving yourself remains the same: you must believe that you have been forgiven." This belief can reinforce your desire and commitment to move on. Privately saying or thinking some mantra that's as simple as "*I am a capable leader*" can become a daily practice. It can serve as a useful reminder of what's right about you in the present, instead of what's gone wrong in the past. It can also inspire you to work on minimizing innate flaws, which can only be mitigated, not necessarily deleted, from the unique code of characteristics that comprises *you*.

Don't be critical of others. People who are hard on themselves are often harsh on others, so watch out for this type of critical tendency. Go a little easy on the people around you. Try to reel in judging thoughts. Think before you speak. Consider how you can be gentler toward others so that your mindset of forgiveness extends beyond you. If what you're about to say isn't truly useful or supportive, realize that whatever you are about to say could become your next big mistake.

In Summary: The Disciplined Leader agrees with many famous and tenacious inventors that failures are opportunities wrapped up like gifts for all of us to open. When it comes to truly understanding mistakes that you've made in your life, realize how each can be an opportunity for building strength and smarts. Focus on discovering the lesson behind what's gone wrong.

Take Action!

✓ Discuss mistakes with friends or colleagues and ask them what you could have done differently.

✓ When you make mistakes, write down thoughts, feelings, and lessons learned in a journal.

✓ Stop the vicious cycle of replaying your mistakes in your head and focus on corrective actions for the future. Forgive yourself.

Listen More, Talk Less

In writing about this topic, I couldn't help but feel a little apprehensive about how my wife Robin would rate me on my ability to listen more and talk less. The need to address my listening skills has been a constant theme in our marriage—an area for improvement in which, let's hope, I've gotten better!

Likewise, in terms of my professional career, my communication skills have needed work over the years, particularly when I was a bit younger. Specifically, to successfully manage people and build relationships, I needed to listen more to others and talk less about myself. As soon as I started making this shift, I became much more aware of what was really going on around me—as if I were seeing work and life in a totally new light. I also learned many new things about people and the organization as a whole. It was incredibly empowering. Yet the real light bulb moment came after I joined MAP and noticed how its consultants are quite proficient in the art of asking good questions and purposefully use this skill whenever they're coaching clients. Rather than give advice, they ask smart questions, knowing that this coaching style is much more powerful for learning, developing, and generating sustainable change. In alignment with the premise of this book, they practice the 80/20 Rule with this habit, listening 80 percent of the time and talking or asking good questions 20 percent of the time. In doing so, MAP consultants really learn what's going on with our clients and can better craft solutions to meet their needs.

There's no doubt leaders like to talk. But great leaders know one of the keys to effective leadership is suppressing the innate desire to hear oneself speak to create that golden opportunity to listen more and talk less. If you're finding yourself doing most of the talking with your direct reports or at meetings, maybe it's time for a change. Piping down and practicing the 80/20 Rule will likely transform your workplace into a more transparent, productive one. Employees, now encouraged to share more ideas and solutions, will have a new platform to speak up and share their thoughts. Consequently, this newfound opportunity will enable them to become more engaged, effective, and energized. When this happens, it can transform your people and your leadership impact for the better.

But common myths exist about talking and leadership— and for whatever reason, people routinely tend to believe them. So here, I'm going to expand my points on listening more and talking less, outlining three common myths and how to respond in spite of them.

Myth #1: As the leader, you're the answer person. True, you might have a lot of good answers or ideas about what works best, how business should be done, solutions to problems, and so on. But The Disciplined Leader encourages employees to look to themselves for the answers. When your team doesn't come up with their own answers, the result is missed opportunities. They don't develop professionally or take ownership of their responsibilities. So, hard as it may be at times, try holding back on providing all the answers, all the time. Challenge your team to come up with the answers and solutions.

Myth #2: Talking makes you interesting. Really? Speaking five languages, being an Olympian, and having the ability to stand on your head makes you interesting. But talking too much? Nope. That only makes you a bore. And you'll know you're a bona fide bore if you catch people rolling their eyes or staring at their phone when you're talking too much in a meeting. If you really want to come across as interesting, try not talking so much the next time you're face to face with someone. Ask compelling questions and only speak up if you have something truly unique or important to add. For instance, have you ever been in meetings where most people are taking their turns at talking except for one person? What happened next? When everyone finishes, that one person offers a startling, one-sentence analysis that turned the meeting on its head, surprising everyone at the conference table. Be that startling silent type once in a while.

Myth #3: Asking good questions comes naturally. Being able to ask good questions is a learned skill that takes discipline and practice to master. When you do this, it fosters discovery, unearthing things that are more meaningful. Asking the right questions can also accelerate your knowledge and leadership potential. Listening is a key part of the equation. Whenever people decide they want to be better listeners, they often think all they need to do is keep their mouths closed. Not true. Good listening is active listening, where you're processing what's being said for the purpose of learning.

In Summary: The Disciplined Leader realized long ago that the best information comes from the best questions. Listening more and then asking probing questions is the fastest way to grow understanding and get the right answers.

Sometimes starting with "I've got to ask a dumb question ... what does X mean?" can yield what psychologists call deep structures of information.

Take Action!

✓ In the next two meetings you attend, practice the 80/20 Rule (listening 80 percent of the time and talking or asking good questions 20 percent of the time).

✓ When dealing with a problem, ask others for their recommended solutions even if you think you have the answer. Be the devil's advocate who can get active discussion and open debate going.

✓ Practice active listening by asking the right questions and playing back the responses to people you interact with this week.

Manage Your Time

As a leader, there may be times when you feel like you're going through the motions of your job and life, completing one task after another with no end in sight. Maybe you find yourself reminiscing about "the good old days" when you actually had time to think, dream, or just breathe. If so, you're not alone. The habit of overcommitting and overscheduling yourself with must-do activities creates a dangerous trap into which leaders commonly fall. Suddenly, you realize you have no energy, no enthusiasm—you're practically inert, and it's all your own doing.

When you're pressed, stressed, and understandably working hard toward achieving your vital goals, you're not going to be at your best. You'll miss out on what others are doing around you because you're too wrapped up in what you've got going on. You may also lose your sense of self, perhaps sacrificing once-important dreams, health, and well-being. Being too busy can also create the perception you're not capable of truly treating yourself right. You'll make mistakes, and direct reports may then question your credibility and durability as a leader.

Smart leaders who've learned the discipline of not over-committing and leaving themselves with free time are ulti-mately more effective, balanced, and in-control of their life. If you're going to be successful at carving out that much-needed free time, you will need to take on some new habits that di-rectly support this goal. Here are a few I recommend:

Attack your calendar. Start looking more closely at what you have on tap for the day, week, or month. Look for opportunities to balance your calendar and open up that much-needed free time. Look for entire days during the month when you can completely block out meet-ings. Also, look at how your free time is being unnec-essarily used for work purposes. For example, if you are currently working during your time off from work, are there corrective actions you can take to get the work done during the regular work week? Good time man-agement can prevent you from shifting gears away from family and friends because you have work you need to finish. The key here is to be proactive and not allow everything that's going on in the world control your calendar.

Create a "To Stop" list. If you're struggling with time management and feeling overwhelmed by The Trivial Many, it's time to create a "To Stop" list. Include ac-tivities on your list that aren't vital to your professional and personal goals and that can either be terminated or delegated. Consider involving your staff members in helping you develop this list by asking for their input. You may have team members who are happy to step up and assume more responsibility to improve their own skills. However you go about doing it, if you lose what lacks real value, you will free up more time to focus on The Vital Few.

Realize "leading doesn't mean always doing." I used to think that if I was really busy, I was somehow proving my value to others. I would pride myself on having back-to-back meetings just to demonstrate how productive I was. In my mind, people would perceive I was working hard and in control. Then I noticed my firm's senior managers—who always seemed cool, calm, and collected—never appeared as busy as I was. How could that be? It took me awhile, but I finally got it: Being busy doesn't mean you're more effective. And it certainly doesn't translate to being in control and confident. If you're guilty of thinking you must always look or be busy, put on the brakes immediately. Develop and use that "To Stop" list and quit thinking you must be the person who says yes to everything and everyone. That's not your role as a leader. Your role is to lead with purpose, wisdom, and command.

In Summary: The Disciplined Leader knows not to overcommit to people and activities in order to maintain a balance between work and free time. Your leadership style will reflect a greater sense of confidence and control if you strike this balance.

Take Action!

✓ Build personal activities into your work calendar so you understand the big picture of what your total time commitment is. Schedule meetings (aka "free time") with yourself and hold firm to this commitment to give yourself more free time.

✓ Cut your meeting time over the next month. Stay more focused and on-topic in meetings. Eliminate unnecessary agenda items that could be addressed outside the meeting.

✓ Develop strategies to say "no" in a positive way to activities you don't need to be doing.

Tackle the
Tough Stuff

Procrastination can be a real killer when it comes to leading yourself effectively. According to *Psychology Today*, 20 percent of people are chronic procrastinators.[5] They avoid challenging tasks or addressing big issues, even seeking out opportunities for distraction. Procrastination has defeating consequences—some direct, some indirect. These negatives can be tangible, like a missed deadline, as well as intangible, such as irritability from losing sleep over an issue. It's an enemy that undermines you, your team, and your company's potential to succeed. Procrastination promotes failure, which can have a serious impact on your organization, its people, and your career as a Disciplined Leader.

At MAP, we work with many leaders who struggle with tackling the tough stuff first. When they lack the experience and confidence needed to do some work activity, they procrastinate, pushing the activity to the back burner. For example, sometimes they put off conversations with their poor-performing employees because they're not confident they'll communicate the feedback effectively. We coach these leaders to overcome this challenge because it's essential to getting the results they need—those tied to their vital goals.

Do you ever avoid meeting with a direct report who isn't performing well, telling yourself you'll get to it later? Or do you tend to postpone intimidating projects that will test your self-confidence, abilities, comfort zone, or patience? If so, those are a few of the classic red flags of procrastination. The following approaches can help you tackle your tough stuff with greater gusto and better manage any procrastination-prone behaviors:

Identify your triggers. A good way to approach this habit is through a self-analysis that reveals activities you are prone to put off. Once you know what your biggest challenges are, try to identify why you procrastinate. Gaining self-awareness will assist you in making positive changes by enabling you to see when and how you're falling into this trap. This exercise will help you recognize your triggers in real time. Moving forward, you will be better equipped to respond in a proactive way and get things done.

Hold yourself accountable. If you know what you procrastinate about, establish a personal accountability system for overcoming this bad habit. For example, when a tough challenge surfaces, put together a small action plan and assign a deadline for getting it done. Then block out a specific time on your calendar to make it happen. Putting the tough issue on your calendar will help prevent procrastination, empowering you to address rather than dodge difficult situations.

Take the first step. There's an old proverb that says, "The hardest part of any journey is taking that first step." If you just get started on something you are putting off, you can break the whole cycle of procrastination. When I procrastinate, I find that 90 percent of the time, whatever I am avoiding is never as bad as I think it will be. What's more, putting off whatever it is brings about a lot of unnecessary stress. Does this sound familiar to you?

If so, take that first step to deal with it, and you will be closer to completing your activity and further from procrastination. Simply by taking on the problem in this manageable, step-by-step way, you will quickly free up valuable, much-needed emotional and mental currency.

In Summary: The Disciplined Leader believes tackling the tough stuff in life and work is an attribute and key indicator of success. Addressing issues head on and avoiding procrastination gives you the power to solve problems quickly so you can focus your time and energy on your Vital Few.

Take Action!

✓ When developing your daily plan, identify the areas or activities you tend to put off. Look for a time of day, day of the week, or any other sort of pattern tied to your procrastination. Schedule these activities first.

✓ Take on difficult challenges earlier in the day when your mind is more focused and you have more energy.

✓ Understand why you procrastinate with certain activities. If you don't know how to do it, seek advice and resources to help you.

Plan Each Day

You may be familiar with the concept that life is two-thirds planning and one-third delivery. Without question, this thinking about the importance of planning holds true in business. That's because, as the well-known time-management author Alan Lakein says, "Failing to plan is planning to fail." Many reasons or excuses exist for why you might fail to plan: You're too busy. Too tired. Too stressed. Or you don't know how or where to start.

Whatever your reasons for not tapping into the power of planning, you need to overcome them. Planning is a disciplined aspect of management that forms needed direction. Planning helps you plot out the best strategies and actions for achieving your vital goals and how to overcome foreseeable obstacles.

In the next lesson, you will receive guidance for a professional development plan that can shape your future. To execute it well, you've got to become a disciplined planner on a daily basis. That said, some people view planning as an event that happens sporadically, on an as-needed basis or as a one-time event. But nothing could be further from the truth. Making plans to attack your daily responsibilities will create the focus you need to manage your time and get more done.

Here is a case in point. Early in my career, I struggled with my daily planning. I'd get into the office without any real road-map for the day. After work, I'd get home and find myself all stressed out, thinking nonstop about all the things I had to do the next day. I spent many a restless night, tossing and turning in bed and going through the mental list of tomorrow's to-dos, trying to remember everything I needed to do. Also, I was worrying about what I was forgetting and plotting out in my tired brain how I would get everything done. It was exhausting and far from productive. To remedy this, I got into the self-discipline of creating a mini-plan of action for each day. This took the thoughts out of my head and put them on paper.

It's likely that you've wrestled with this same demon in your past. The good news is planning to attack tomorrow can alleviate anxiety and put your mind at rest today. Don't obsess over devising any sort of plan in great detail—it doesn't need to be rocket science. Just taking a few minutes to jot down a daily plan of attack can suffice.

Below are several expanded points around disciplining yourself to plan regularly so you can turn your scattered ways into saner days:

Establish daily goals. At the close of each workday, develop your "Top Three" goals for the next day. These should be broad in nature and reflective of your general leadership responsibilities, such as "plan the offsite meeting," "set up three interviews for current job vacancy," or "choose new benefits plan." This is a simple and powerful exercise because it gives you the direction and focus you'll need to have a successful day. Over the years, many of MAP's clients have told us that they are most productive the day before they go on vacation. They come into work knowing they have to get things done, and because of their motivation to go on vacation, they make it happen. The same principle applies here.

Set goals for the day, make a commitment to get them done, and you'll be more likely to accomplish them. Consider the day successful if you meet only these goals.

Create your "activity hit list." In addition to developing your goals, start creating a daily list of work activities for the following day. As mentioned, the sheer act of putting these items on paper will be what gets them out of your mind, where they are just randomly rolling around. Once you have your activities down on paper, prioritize how you will tackle these items the following day.

Review your calendar. Daily planning wouldn't be complete without reviewing your calendar. It is important to understand what you have scheduled, and an instant review of this provides a snapshot of what appointments and meetings are scheduled. Since nothing can throw your day off quicker than being unprepared for a meeting or forgetting about a commitment, this exercise will free you from needing to remember in the evening what's on schedule for the next day.

In Summary: The Disciplined Leader creates a daily plan to increase productivity and goal achievement. It's on the desk or computer each evening and ready for the morning. Attack each day with a predetermined direction to accomplish more and reduce stress.

Take Action!

✓ Review your plan at the start of each morning and keep it visible throughout the day. Make sure those set priorities are still in alignment with what needs to happen.

✓ Challenge yourself to shrink your daily list of activities by 25 percent by looking for items you can delegate.

✓ Track your progress and hold yourself accountable. Cross off completed activities to give yourself a sense of accomplishment.

Write Your Professional Development Plan

Imagine boarding an old cruise ship setting sail to your favorite destination. As you board the vessel with your loved ones, you are warmly greeted by the crew and staff. You locate your cabin and check out your accommodations. Everything is perfect. You quickly head to the higher deck for a quick toast and to wave bon voyage. You can't wait for the cast off to sail straight toward your destination. But then the captain comes on the PA system and announces that the cruise is cancelled because he's discovered the ship has lost its rudder. Without a rudder, there is no way to steer the ship.

Like a ship without a rudder, many of us go through life without any real direction or solid definition of what we want to accomplish. In fact, we spend more time researching and planning for our vacations than our future. But having a professional development plan—a blueprint for where we want to go, what we want to be, and the steps we need to take to achieve it—can make the difference between professional fulfillment and failure. Just like a business plan, your professional development plan should include goals and strategies for success.

A solid, yet regularly updated development plan is not only empowering; it fosters discipline for what you want to achieve. It's a tool that takes you one step closer toward transformative experiences and results.

You're busy—I get it. But you did find time to read this book, so you are clearly motivated to grow and develop. Therefore, after reading this lesson, carve out time to develop a draft of your plan that will get you off to a great start. At work, we create business plans for business. At home, we design financial plans with our spouse. In sports, we develop game plans. All share a common goal—the desire for success. If you want to be a Disciplined Leader, crafting a plan is paramount to success. Formulate your professional development plan with the following in mind:

Write out your plan. The very first step is to determine your professional development goals. In working with thousands of managers, our organization always asks this vital planning question first: "What's the goal?" This is important for leading your organization and team, but it's also essential for leading yourself. It forces you to address what you're trying to do, where you want to be, and what your future destination will be. Why does that matter? It's part of Disciplined Leadership. In my experience, the most Disciplined Leaders have been self-driven, lifelong learners who always put their goals down on paper and assigned a timeline with action steps for accomplishing those goals. They remained personally accountable to whatever they were pushing themselves to learn, do, or achieve.

When it comes to creating a development plan, the exact words or perfect format is not what's important. What matters most is the activity for taking control of your growth by writing your plan. I've provided a template that you're free to use here. But you are welcome to write your own plan in a different format.

Share your plan. Once you develop a draft of your plan, I recommend sharing it with a trusted advisor. This may be the same person with whom you've confided regarding other practices in this first part, but he or she should be able to give you input on your plan and what you want to accomplish. Preferably this person has experience with self-development and growth, understanding what the opportunities are, and foreseeing obstacles you may encounter. Pick a mentor with good coaching skills—someone who will patiently guide you in decision making.

Make it a living document. Some people go through the planning process and then let their plan collect dust on a shelf. This is the last thing you want to do. Make sure that after you've drawn up your plan, you're not just using it but periodically reviewing, updating, and revising it. What you initially write won't always be perfect. But get into this routine, and you'll find that plan is more relevant, accurate, and useful in the long run.

In Summary: The Disciplined Leader has a professional development plan. It is the blueprint, the ship's rudder, to ensure the right destination is reached. It includes the steps needed to reach the destination. Having this plan is the catalyst for your success—it can make the difference between your professional fulfillment or failure.

Take Action!

✓ Make a dedicated commitment to develop your written plan. Write it down to make it real, give it "legs," and enable direction. Any format will work. Just get the words on paper, not worrying if it's perfect.

✓ Assign due dates to your planned activities to create greater structure and accountability. One way to do this is to "backcast," that is, start with the ultimate goal and its desired completion date, and work backward to subordinate goals and their desired completion dates.

✓ Find a confidant or mentor who has the right experience to guide you with objectivity and skill as you map your plan.

PROFESSIONAL DEVELOPMENT PLAN	

Name:_____   Date:_____

1.   Current Situation:_____

Professional Motivators   MOTIVATORS

• _____

• _____

• _____

Strengths	Opportunities	STRENGTHS & OPPORTUNITIES
1. _____	1. _____	
2. _____	2. _____	
3. _____	3. _____	
4. _____	4. _____	

Mentor(s):_____   MENTORS

Coach(es):_____   COACHES

Professional Growth Barriers   GROWTH BARRIERS

• _____

• _____

• _____

Figure 3 *Professional Development Plan*

2. Professional Growth Goals:

GOAL #1   A. Professional Development Goal: _____

_____

ACTION STEPS

	Action Steps	When
1.	_____	_____
2.	_____	_____
3.	_____	_____
4.	_____	_____

MEASUREMENTS   Measurements I will use to know that I have achieved this goal:

_____

_____

_____

GOAL #2   B. Professional Development Goal: _____

_____

ACTION STEPS

	Action Steps	When
1.	_____	_____
2.	_____	_____
3.	_____	_____
4.	_____	_____

MEASUREMENTS   Measurements I will use to know that I have achieved this goal:

_____

_____

_____

Figure 3 *Professional Development Plan (continued)*

3. Strategies to maximize my performance:

- _____   **MAXIMIZING STRATEGIES**
- _____
- _____
- _____

4. Key elements I have learned about my leadership style that impact my performance and/or development:

Style Elements to Consider in My Development   **STYLE ELEMENTS**

- _____
- _____
- _____
- _____

5. Accountability strategies to ensure I follow through on my development:

Accountability Strategies	**Frequency**	**ACCOUNTABILITY STRATEGIES**
1. _____	_____	
2. _____	_____	
3. _____	_____	
4. _____	_____	

Figure 3 *Professional Development Plan (continued)*

6.   Career Goal:

GOAL #1   A.   Professional Development Goal:_____

_____

ACTION STEPS

Action Steps   **When**

1. _____   _____

2. _____   _____

3. _____   _____

4. _____   _____

MEASUREMENTS   Measurements I will use to know that I have achieved this goal:

_____

_____

_____

Figure 3 *Professional Development Plan (continued)*

Believe in
Your Potential

When you're rock climbing and can see what you need to grasp and where you need to go, there's only one thing that has the potential to hold you back: your lack of faith in yourself. You have to call upon your courage and zero in on exactly what you want as you move upward and onward to that place of greater security, stability, and success. As you make that leap toward your goal, there will be a moment in which you're touching nothing. Yet you know that if you position yourself correctly before you start, move just right, and fuel yourself with bravery, energy, and intention, you'll transition with greater ease; and odds are, you'll reach your mark. You simply have to believe.

One afternoon, a MAP client called his consultant and cheerfully announced that he had the perfect answer for how to manage his business effectively: He would hire his MAP consultant to take over and run it for him. Immediately recognizing that this was really a case of classic self-doubt, the consultant explained to this highly capable leader that it's the consultant's job to coach their clients how to do their job—not to do the job for them. This leader had put all the measures in place for success; he just had to believe in himself. In the end, he did and went on to become a strategic execution expert and highly esteemed business leader who turned his $10 million business into a $40 million business within a ten-year time frame.

And so, too, must you simply believe as you develop the best habits for supporting your leadership challenge and building your capacity for influence. You've completed an enormous amount of introspective work and have what you need to start on and succeed with the next part of your leadership journey. Self-confidence is essential for success, specifically, believing in your ability to focus on The Vital Few and taking the steps to move forward. As you prepare to take those steps, remember to do the following:

Ignore negative self-talk. Maybe as you're reading this lesson, you're recognizing you need to do a better job believing in your potential. One of the big challenges we all face when trying to focus on our positive attributes is the self-doubt that is driven by negative self-talk. Research has shown that we do a lot of negative self-talk every day. We can be our own worst critics when it comes to believing in our potential because as humans we tend to focus on our flaws rather than our potential. To accelerate your growth, monitor and manage any form of self-doubt, which, if unchecked, can easily creep back into your mind and thwart positive intentions.

Manage external negativity. We all have relationships with individuals who bring negative energy into our lives. I'm sure there are people in your life who come to mind and fit into this category. If you're spending any significant time with them, odds are, they are bringing you down. The worst offenders are the ones who make efforts to point out your weaknesses, flaws, and mistakes. So I recommend completely eliminating or drastically reducing the time you spend with them.

That said, it's sometimes hard in life to just stop having a relationship with somebody—but you have the capability to control your attitude and how this person affects you.

Nurture what you've cultivated. To increase your odds of leadership success, take care of yourself physically, mentally, and emotionally so that you have the energy to make positive change. Be realistic and expect an imperfect journey. But always believe in a fulfilling experience regardless of any imperfections.

In Summary: The Disciplined Leader knows how to acknowledge shortcomings and overcome them with a working plan. Believing in your potential and calling upon your courage to change will fuel your professional growth and help you accomplish goals.

Take Action!

✓ Identify the areas where you lack confidence and why you lack confidence. Make sure these areas are included in your development plan.

✓ Review the list of things you already do well in prior lessons and reflect on them whenever you need a reminder or boost.

✓ Fake it 'til you make it. Adopt a confident style and recognize that at times you have to be a bit of an actor until your confidence increases.

Wrap-up

In this first part of the book, I've offered you a lot of tips about how to focus on leading yourself. You've explored who you are as a leader, including your strengths, weaknesses, values, and possible opportunities to improve your leadership style. You've learned you need courage to become a Disciplined Leader, as well as willpower to commit to change, tear down stubborn barriers, create a better work-life balance, and believe in your power to achieve your vital goals. You also now know your company's most vital asset is your people, and that includes and starts with you. At the heart of winning organizations and teams are Disciplined Leaders who are great at leading themselves, and that's ultimately what influences how well they lead their teams and the organization as a whole.

I hope you've realized that you are unique, as is your leadership journey in becoming The Disciplined Leader. To reach that destination, what you need to address and the efforts you must make will also be unique. No other leader will follow the same path and tackle challenges exactly as you do. And that's OK.

If you haven't already done so, it's now time for you to browse back through the chapters and create that list of your "Top Three" Vital Few—the mindsets and habits you'll focus on from Part I. Once you've identified your Vital Few, write them down in the *Vital Few Template* we've provided on pages 7–8.

If you're like me, it's quite possible you're feeling *all* these tips in Part I are vital to leading yourself, one of the three core areas of your leadership responsibility. And you are right. For the record, they *are* all important. But since this book is designed to help you identify and take action around your Vital Few, choose what's most important for you to improve in this area of your leadership. The following questions may help:

- Which few tips speak to your most serious leadership barriers or weaknesses?

- Which few habits or mindsets could make the biggest difference in your leadership style today?

- Which few tips can you leverage to make the greatest effect and enable you to be a more Disciplined Leader overall?

Once you've got your Vital Few selected, let's move on to Part II.

Part II

Break Through and Get Results

The Responsibility to Lead Your Team

In working through the first part of the book, you identified your Vital Few in relationship to your first core area of leadership: the responsibility to lead yourself. Now, we're going to build on that bedrock of learning through a number of tips tied to the second core area of leadership: the responsibility to lead your team.

Think of your team as the link between you and your entire organization. Those who are working closely with you are an extension of your leadership style. As you model certain behaviors, those on your team learn effective strategies for management and professional self-discipline that connect to and strengthen the entire organization. You count on them to help you achieve your goals. You need them to help in ways that support your commitment to your Vital Few. Therefore, you need to lead your team and develop those on it in a way that's fair, constructive, and inspiring. That's how you will motivate and fuel your team to perform, produce, and drive sustainable results.

Why does this matter? Do a poor job leading your team and fail to focus on improving this area of leadership, and you'll never win in business—at least in the long run. Your team might occasionally score random successes, but consistent victory will be impossible to achieve. The team, suffering from negligent or misfired leadership, will be weak. Eventually, that weakness will give way, resulting in greater business vulnerability and failure.

It's every leader's responsibility to lead and build the team in a way that strengthens and supports it. MAP spends the bulk of its time, both in its 2.5 day executive workshop and its consulting services, coaching around this topic. Steering clear of management fads or new trends, we focus on business fundamentals around the key functions of management. We concentrate on empowering leaders to drive better performance by building strategies that engage and align their teams—because that's what they need most.

To drive performance and get your goals accomplished, you've got to have a team of people who work well as individuals, together, and with you. Specifically, these individuals must respect you and respond favorably to your leadership. They must remain motivated through a system that's rooted in fundamental ways to develop, perform, produce, and deliver against key goals. They must also be capable of taking on more responsibility to fuel their growth and give you the opportunity to remain focused on your main leadership duties, including your vital asset—your people.

Reading through these tips, keep in mind you need to select your Vital Few at this part's end. Before you get going, jot down five challenges you're having in regard to leading your team. As you go through each tip in this area of development, see if any of these topics address the issues you're facing. After you're done, there's a good chance that these mindsets and habits just might be your "Top Three" Vital Few for this part.

#20

Choose the Right Words

As Mark Twain once put it, "The difference between the right word and almost the right word is the difference between lightning and a lightning bug." The power of the spoken word is so important. If you implement all the good habits in this book but regularly mess up on this one, it could threaten your ability to lead your team, perhaps even derail your career.

During one of our monthly Vital Factor team meetings, a client proudly proclaimed he wanted his company to look like an automobile perfectly prepped and ready for sale. When the meeting ended, his MAP consultant pulled him aside and asked him if he was planning to sell his business. "No," replied the client. "I was just trying to sound inspirational in using that particular example."

"Well, now you've got a recovery effort on your hands because of how your words came across to everyone sitting in the room," his consultant cautioned. "Your people think you're planning to sell the company and now they need to look for a new job. It doesn't matter if you think what you said sounded right because what they think you said *is* all that really matters."

As business-management expert Tom Peters once said, "Perception is all there is." Political pollster and wordsmith Frank Luntz, in his book *Words That Work*, warns it's not what you say; it's what people hear.

When you discipline yourself to choose the right words, gradually this practice feels less forced and even second nature. Such communication is really an art; yet as with all forms of artistry, there's always a learning curve and loads of practice involved. But the end result can be a masterpiece in terms of managing your communication effectively and excelling at achieving your vision.

You're challenged every day to choose the right words to communicate on matters both serious and trite. From a fundamental standpoint, it is important to your leadership reputation to carefully select what you say and how you say it, making sure what you say truly aligns to the values you defined earlier. When your communication is compelling and clear, and it consistently reflects your values, you will be more likely to build respect and improve teamwork.

Here is what you'll find this great habit can do:

Inspire your team. When your team members understand exactly what you want and hear your consistent, genuine passion, they'll believe you and be more likely to get behind your goals. To keep your communication genuine, choose words you would honestly say, and your authenticity will show. Inflammatory expressions or foul language can undermine communication effectiveness or unknowingly fuel hostility.

Give your vision life. When you're communicating important business matters, plan what you're going to say to your team. The last thing you want to do is appear unsure, inconsistent, uninterested, or disengaged. Employees will pick up on it right away. Ineffectively communicating your vision is poor leadership personified. Being specific about the who, what, where, and when of the vision transforms it from a wish into a realistic idea. With buy-in, it can take form and be acted upon by your team.

Create awesome energy in the workplace. Everyone needs positive energy whenever possible! Pick words that fuel action, lift spirits, and make people feel competent. Such "can-do" words can seemingly work miracles. They can build trust, demonstrate honesty, instigate action, clarify meanings, strengthen teams, express kindness, and reflect empathy. Weigh communications with words that are positive and productive in nature, avoiding the overuse of negative words and slang. Try not to conjure up feelings, thoughts, or implications that unnecessarily zap the enthusiasm out of your team members and your workplace.

In Summary: The Disciplined Leader knows not only the importance of words that are used but also the larger importance of how people hear those words. Choose the right words and say the right things. Doing so can inspire your team, sell your ideas, and create energy in the workplace.

Take Action!

✓ Think before you speak. Prepare for important communications and conversations, planning and practicing what you're going to say.

✓ Practice a communication style that reflects your values and a high level of professionalism. Discontinue any off-color jokes, swearing, or other careless language behaviors.

✓ Don't say something if you have any doubts. Rethink your message and then speak.

Put Your Game Face on

Many of the lessons in this part are focused on your leadership style and specifically address communication patterns. Communication is not just about what you say and write to your team. Nonverbal communication is a very powerful medium as well. For example, you could probably take a snapshot of people's faces at work and be able to tell which day is a Monday and which is a Friday because the way they feel is reflected through their body language. Also, you can detect when someone is disagreeing with you even though that individual isn't saying so outright. How do you know? Poor eye contact or a slight frown, perhaps. It's the body language that ultimately is speaking volumes—and quite loudly at times—about what's really going on with that individual's thoughts and feelings.

Leaders tend to pay way more attention to their verbal communication than their nonverbal communication. Many leaders often aren't aware of what their nonverbal habits are and how they regularly affect others. At MAP, part of our workshop involves videotaping our participants talking about a particular topic. Then we show it to them. The majority of participants are surprised how their body language can undermine what they're saying verbally.

In business and, specifically, working closely with your team, it's really helpful to understand the importance of non-verbal communication. One of the most widely cited studies on verbal versus nonverbal messages shows that up to 55 percent of communication effectiveness is in facial expression and body language in general.[6] What this means is that body language doesn't lie and can make or break what and how well you communicate to others. Realizing its power can radically improve your ability to spot communication challenges with your people, give you an opportunity to address workplace transparency, and perfect your own communication style.

It's sometimes difficult to hide feelings when we are dealing with hard situations or personal circumstances that are bothering us. But good leaders learn how to manage this. They know how to mask their feelings when appropriate and not portray their internal emotions through their body language. Masking your feelings isn't about being fake toward others, lying, or being otherwise dishonest. It is about controlling your emotions and thinking before you speak. It's about maintaining the display of verbal cues that say, "I'm in control" and "I'm open to what you have to say even though I may or may not agree." It's about learning to keep your game face on.

What messages are you sending? Where do you need to take corrective action? Since you've got a million other things to do in your leadership development and because it would obviously be a full-time job to constantly monitor your body language, try focusing on what nonverbal cues you're communicating to your team, particularly in the following scenarios or situations:

Check "Monday blues" at the door. Many people don't love Mondays. But because leadership sets the tone, you really want to lose that classic "Monday morning blues" look when it's your turn to arrive at the office. Why? Emotions are contagious, and people will notice. Pay attention to the person in the mirror, and you will have a positive impact on your direct reports, peers, and boss. Make this a daily activity until it becomes a habit.

Correct nonverbal disengagement in meetings. Want to observe some solid, high levels of disengagement communicated through nonverbal messages? Meetings provide the perfect opportunity. Participants think that they're not being observed if they're not talking. But nothing could be further from the truth. In fact, it's so common that our senior MAP consultants coach our clients on paying attention to body language—both their own and that of others. They learn how to gain awareness about who is engaged and who isn't, too. For example, maybe the sales manager is avoiding eye contact. His being "checked out" in the meeting is a red flag, and you need to find out what's going on.

Watch emotions amid personal crisis. If you're in business long enough, you're going to run into situations where you've got to go to work even though you're dealing with a personal issue that's extremely emotional. I'm not saying it's easy to shut your emotions off, but do your best to manage them. This starts with being conscientious about what you want to display. Just keeping it together and not wearing your heart on your sleeve for everyone to see can help. Some people are better at this than others, but I would encourage you to maintain composure. When really tough, personal times arrive, you will be more experienced and well-practiced for dealing with those while you are at work.

In Summary: The Disciplined Leader knows nonverbal communication (gestures, eyes, arms, stance, attentiveness) can overpower anything said. Nonverbal communication sends messages that speak to the whole person and influence your ability to build effective relationships with your team, influence those individuals, and lead your people overall.

Take Action!

✓ Video yourself talking or presenting to others. Play it back and observe your nonverbal communication cues. Note the good, the bad, and the ugly about what you see.

✓ Check yourself before going into the office. Set a goal to reflect confidence and put your game face on.

✓ Demonstrate engagement in meetings through positive verbal cues, such as good eye contact, uncrossed arms, playing back what others say, and other types of body language.

Be in the Moment

Zeroing in on your Vital Few demands focus. One the ways you can quickly get greater focus is by being in the moment. It forces you to be present and fully committed to what's before you. Moreover, being in the moment with your team, those you must regularly influence in your leadership, will boost your ability to lead effectively and ultimately drive better results.

That's why MAP consultants often make it a rule in their monthly accountability meeting with clients to have everyone turn off electronics. These are time robbers as is multitasking in other ways during meetings. Checking email or texting in such accountability meetings means you are focused on The Trivial Many, not The Vital Few. In fact, one MAP consultant even puts a basket in the middle of the table so everyone gathered for the meeting can toss in their cell phones.

It's no surprise that people struggle to part with their technology and be fully present at first. Leaders often resist because they think they always need to be connected and know what's going on with everything, at all times. But deep down, everyone knows being fully engaged is for the best.

In fact, you've probably had a meeting when your team members kept looking at their computer screens or texting in the middle of your conversation. How did that make you feel? Chances are, not so good. No matter how commonplace and seemingly acceptable such technology-related behaviors are today, everyone's inattention and inability to remain present with you probably made you feel like you and the subject matter were unimportant.

You probably know people who are terrible at "being in the moment"—and maybe you are one of them. A leader like this is preoccupation personified, the classic White Rabbit who is always running around, allegedly late for some "very important date" with no time to say "hello, goodbye"—just, "I'm late, I'm late, I'm late!" Or maybe this leader stops to say hello, but doesn't really take the time to listen, learn how you're doing, and engage your thoughts and opinions in some meaningful way. Instead, this individual dominates the conversation by talking about himself. Perhaps this person appears to listen but demonstrates other communication cues (toe tapping, inching toward the door, sighing) that say, "This meeting is only about going through the motions."

When leaders do this or have other "I'm preoccupied" behaviors, they make the people on their team feel as if they're undervalued. Over time, that behavior can damage their ability to build good relationships with those individuals as well as others. This hurts team spirit, productivity, and the bottom line. People tend to think such leaders are too busy at best, self-absorbed at worst.

But there's no denying that the world *is* a busy place. Everyone has a demanding life to lead, and you can't always put aside distractors and ignore what happened yesterday or what's coming down the pipeline tomorrow. You're continually challenged to juggle it all while succeeding in your job, which makes "being in the moment" downright tough sometimes. But lean into the discomfort and trust that it will be okay. When it comes to leading your team, it's your responsibility to remain fully present. This takes serious self-discipline, but it will make a difference in your relationships and your ability to achieve goals and get results.

To practice getting more in the moment with your team, consider these tactics:

> **Give yourself a pep talk.** Every morning, do a personal pep talk and inspire yourself to "be in the moment" in regard to the interactions you'll have throughout the day. You can do the same kind of cheerleading when it comes to your relationships outside of work. In fact, a colleague once told me that on his way home from a stressful day at work, he often pulls over, stops the car, and "gets in the moment." When he greets his wife at home, he is engaged, focused, and much more present with her. In fact, being in the moment is one of the secrets to great relationships, friendships, partnerships, and so on, which can net big returns whether you're nurturing them with a team member, staff member, co-worker, customer, friend, or family member. It's good common sense.

> **Eliminate distractions.** In a world in which there are so many distractions, everything from computers to smart-phones and other helpful yet invasive types of technology and media, you've got to be careful about such diversions when you're meeting with people. You see it all the time at work, in restaurants, at sporting events, at parks, and in so many other places. People get sucked into playing with their phones instead of being in the moment with those who are with them. At least at work, you can take some proactive steps to minimize distractions if you're going to be meeting with somebody on your team. For example, if the meeting is in your office, don't sit behind your desk with the computer screen staring at you. Push your chair around and face that person and show you're committed and engaged. When you take such small steps, you will boost your chances of being in the moment and send the message that your audience is important.

Show that you're engaged. When a team member comes to you and tries to share some thoughts, embrace it as an opportunity to practice being in the moment. Remember, this is a human being who is there to connect with you, even support your leadership potential. As my colleague used to do, when you're about to meet with people or have an audience giving you its attention, show them the courtesy of giving them yours. This good habit proves you care, an effort that can go a long way toward transforming your leadership and taking it to a higher level.

In Summary: The Disciplined Leader is attentive in the moment and knows presence is not limited to the physical. The Disciplined Leader considers digital multitasking rude in front of others. Being in the moment is about connecting with your team, building engagement, and showing others they really matter. That means using your eyes and ears and not your thumbs and fingers.

Take Action!

✓ Adopt a rule of no electronic devices during one-to-one meetings. Mute your phone and get out from behind your computer screen to demonstrate your engagement.

✓ Prepare for an upcoming conversation or team meeting within the next week. Set the goal to remain in the moment. Rate your level of success. How well did you meet your goal?

✓ Ask for feedback on your level of engagement after personal interactions.

Focus on What Is Right, Not Who Is Right

It's been my experience in life that people like to be right. My wife Robin tells me, "You know, John, there is nothing you enjoy more in life than being right." I know her insight is spot-on because I've always been that way. There is something about being right that validates how clever and intelligent we are and makes us feel good about ourselves. When it comes to the workplace, the reality is most people have the same desire to be right. But when an individual's need to be right drives decision making and becomes a consistent source of conflict, problems arise.

Over the years, MAP's consultants have witnessed many of its clients and their employees personalize disagreements with one another. Instead of focusing on the problem and the best possible solution, these people have been more invested in their own ideas because they're emotionally attached to them. To add to this consternation, when a problem surfaces under an employee's responsibility, perhaps that individual goes into defensive mode, shifting or refusing to take the blame rather than fixing the problem. This is such a big issue in companies that

MAP coaches its clients to create ground rules for meetings, such as: "Attack the problem, not the person."

In terms of your own leadership, realize that you don't have to be right all the time to demonstrate your competence. In fact, if you're obsessed with trying to show your competence by always being right and trying to win every argument, you will reflect a questionable, less-confident leadership style. Admitting you don't have all the answers takes greater guts. What's more, self-assured, strong leaders will happily change their position if they recognize another person has brought something better to the table. They feel liberated from thinking they must always have the perfect answer to every problem and can spend more of their time and energy doing vital leadership tasks.

To help you develop good practices, consider the following tactics:

Be open to other ideas. If you're going to communicate confidence by not having to be right all the time, you've got to come across as someone who is consistently open to others' ideas. Part of what gives a dynamic workplace that energy is the fact that it's full of people with different opinions to offer the business. For example, let's say you are sharing an idea in a meeting with others, and someone challenges it with what they think is a better solution. When this happens, view this as a chance to reflect a confident leadership style that values openness. Facilitate a meaningful discussion about the other idea, and determine if it has merit or maybe trumps your idea, fair and square.

Admit when you're not right. Let's face it: as much as we want to always be right, it just isn't possible. Robin sometimes takes great delight when I'm wrong and gets a certain playful, yet knowing smirk on her face that I can read a mile away. In business, there can be a huge benefit to admitting that you're wrong in certain situations. Despite that fact, I've worked with plenty of professionals who were afraid to fess up about being wrong.

We'd be in a meeting and that person would be presented with all kinds of facts and qualitative information that would prove their thinking was erroneous. Yet they would still take their stance, dig in their heels, and refuse to give in to any other line of thinking. Politicians do this all the time. Sometimes it can be almost comical and other times pathetic to watch as this behavior plays out because everyone around that person knows the truth. When this happens, people will form an opinion: this person is ignorant, lacks confidence, or both, and also has issues with always needing to be right. More than likely, the behavior will be repeated, and once there's a pattern of behavior, that can erode leadership credibility and respect.

Involve others in your decisions. Many times as a leader, you're ultimately responsible for making decisions and being right. So the challenge is getting the solid answers and solutions before making your final decision. Start by asking people for their input from the get-go. Then involve others as you continue through any decision-making process, allowing them to contribute their ideas and solutions. This approach sends the message you're not afraid to admit you don't have all the answers, all the time, and you understand the value of "group intelligence."

At MAP, we teach a method called Team Consulting. This is a structured method for getting a group of individuals involved in developing solutions to an individual's problem. This overall approach and its process reinforces that you don't have all the answers and your team can help you. When the process is used, it communicates that people require the support of others to make the best decisions and develop the right solutions. It's a great practice for developing the best solutions.

In Summary: The Disciplined Leader knows being right is not always necessary. By releasing the need to be right all the time and consistently searching for the best answer or solution, you will make better decisions. Your leadership style will reflect an openness and confidence that will foster credibility and respect.

Take Action!

✓ Use a "Team Consulting" approach in building solutions to tough problems.

✓ When disagreement occurs, develop a strategy to ask good questions to better understand the other person's point of view.

✓ When discussing a problem or disagreement, go back and get clarity by defining "What's the goal?"

Don't Cross the Line

You can recover from some leadership mistakes. But a recovery effort can be a whole lot tougher if you cross the line in business. As hard as you're working to develop and sustain your reputation as a Disciplined Leader, if you start crossing the line, your professional image and career can get messy.

What do I mean by crossing the line? It is doing something that compromises your leadership position and could threaten your job. Examples include mismanaging your team or violating the ethical standards of your organization. It's a big deal—a common problem that MAP has coached clients on throughout its six decades of consulting.

For instance, whenever someone is suddenly promoted to supervise former coworkers, crossing-the-line challenges can crop up. It's common for coworkers to pressure a newly promoted supervisor to still act like their buddy and be "one of the gang." But whenever a supervisor caves to this pressure and doesn't do the job required, that leader's credibility immediately erodes. Worse, if that supervisor fails to act according to company policy, that individual's job may suddenly be in jeopardy.

Any little slip-up and those coworkers can leverage what's happened to oust their supervisor. It happens all the time.

As one MAP consultant says, there are at least a couple of surefire ways to determine if you've crossed that boss-buddy line. Just ask: If that person stops performing well, can you fire him or her? If the answer is no to that question, then it's likely some boss-buddy line has been crossed—a precarious "point of no return" in any professional environment.

First-level leadership can be a surprisingly tough challenge. After all, you've got to spend 50 percent of your time representing the team and 50 percent of the time managing upwards. But remember, representing your team doesn't mean compromising your authority to drive results and succeed. It means engaging with your team while keeping its best interests at heart, within the framework of your leadership responsibilities.

In addition, you'll probably find that issues around crossing the line may extend well beyond your employees and your boss. It's possible to cross the line with those in any level of your company, even beyond the organization itself, from vendors to your customers and the general public. Keeping that in mind, guard against this trap whenever possible, paying particular attention to these more common scenarios and situations:

> **Boss and employee.** Crossing the line causes confusion. You get confused; your employees get confused. Get too close with someone who reports to you, and the discipline process gets tricky to manage. Employees, thinking your friendship is what's driving their career potential, will get confused when you suddenly have to discipline them and send the message that you are the boss. But you *are* the boss first, and so always reinforce that message through your words and actions. Even when you're socializing with your employees, remain on guard and be careful not to compromise your authority with whatever you say or do.

Customer relationships. Whenever you are dealing with customers, you are representing your organization. But sometimes leaders forget this and make promises that compromise their ethics and betray the organization's rules and values. Maybe they accept gifts from a customer in exchange for price reductions or free products. They may get away with it once or twice, but most leaders who habitually compromise their ethics in this way put their careers in jeopardy.

So whatever the situation, discipline yourself to represent your organization and your team in the best light. If you find yourself in a situation that raises questions around ethics, seek guidance from your boss and remain transparent at all times.

Vendor relationships. Always draw and maintain clear lines in the sand when working with your vendors. Unethical vendors are known for offering free gifts and expensive items to find favor with company decision makers. When dealing with vendors, avoid gifts or promises that could cause a conflict of interest. If approached with something that even hints of violating ethical guidelines, report the incident immediately. It's always better to be safe than sorry.

In Summary: The Disciplined Leader recognizes the boundaries between those above, those below, and those retained. Never be placed in a situation that could compromise your judgment or *appear* to compromise your judgment. Crossing the line weakens your leadership authority and puts your career in jeopardy.

Take Action!

✓ Evaluate your current relationships with your team to determine if you are crossing the line with an individual or the whole team.

✓ Conduct this same type of analysis for any business relationships (vendors, suppliers, consultants) beyond your team and the organization.

✓ Write out corrective actions to fix any identified issues and take action in a timely manner.

Treat Everyone Fairly

You're going to like certain people more than others. It's human nature. But in leadership, don't give preferential treatment to an employee just because you really click with that person. Nothing will get your team's attention faster and erode morale quicker than playing favorites. This game of preferential treatment can build barriers and hostilities, create a mini-culture of exclusivity among your people, and most certainly damage your leadership credibility. Avoid this leadership sin at all costs by consistently treating everyone fairly, always striving to sustain a reputation for being a leader who doesn't play favorites.

The reason playing favorites strikes such a strong chord in people is that it stems from childhood, when we were less mature and intensely impressionable. For example, I went from feeling like a superstar in my second-grade class to an utter failure in third grade. In second grade, my teacher loved me, and everyone knew it. My third grade teacher inexplicably didn't like me, and that was a nightmare. Suddenly, I hated school. But here's the upside: Later in life, I realized the teacher's unfairness was a golden lesson. I learned that exemplary leaders—be they teachers, coaches, parents, or bosses—don't play favorites. Specifically, they:

Avoid the "buddy trap." When you share common interests or really get along with your employee, watch out for the tendency to treat that one worker as the boss's pet. For example, a boss waltzes in every morning, greets his staff quickly, but then always lingers at Jason's desk to talk about the weekend's big game. After work, Jason and the boss take regular bike rides, an activity that's not open to other employees. Then, they're spotted having beers after their ride, and everyone is speculating about what they're discussing, plotting, and planning. In no time, Jason's co-workers feel slighted, inferior, and worried because the boss's actions reflect that they are less valued then their co-worker. It's this kind of favoritism that can have detrimental effects in the workplace. As the leader in your business, take steps to put everyone on the same playing field. Learn to walk the line, maintaining that tricky boss-subordinate balance with everyone you lead.

Focus on teamwork. In sports, great coaches know that flawless teamwork is the key to a winning team. When the magic happens, everybody plays to their fullest potential and gets focused on the collective win. You also need to share this perspective at work. Doing so inspires people to achieve their goals. That's only possible when your team members feel fully and equally empowered to excel, push their potential to the max, and embrace collaboration in the process.

Be consistent and equitable about how you manage others, making it part of your leadership style. For instance, watch out for the tendency to recognize just the same old players for yet another big win. Be equitable about how you dish out praise.

Hold everyone accountable. When it comes to holding people accountable, the last thing you want to do is show preferential treatment with some and inequity with others. Your best tactic: make everyone deliver in ways that are fair yet equally challenging according to the goals and expectations set before them. This sends the message that when it comes to performance, corrective action, results, and even disciplinary measures, you have no favorites—that's not your style. Instead, your management style is one of fairness, accomplished by positively recognizing people based upon the performance they deliver, not just who they are.

In Summary: The Disciplined Leader knows playing favorites can sink morale. Favoritism can knock you off course from your goals because the hint of favoritism will become a major distraction to the team.

Take Action!

✓ Identify if you are playing favorites with any current employees and develop a plan of action to get back across the line.

✓ Document equitable performance expectations for all employees. Be fair and consistent about how you address performance issues and recognize your employees. Spread recognition around, finding opportunities to recognize everyone.

✓ Coach your direct reports around not playing favorites with subordinates. Everyone needs to know that the culture supports equity, not favoritism.

Honor Your Commitments

I had a boss whose favorite mantra was "commitments are sacred." The thing about his mantra was he didn't just talk about it. He also clearly applied it to our entire operations team, including how we worked together and served our customers. Because he was unrelenting and consistent about this mantra, I eventually became a believer.

Honoring your commitments is a high-impact activity that can make or break your entire credibility as a leader. The Disciplined Leader promises only what he or she can do. In the end, such leaders build entire reputations, even legacies, around being known as people who always do what they say they are going to do.

When it comes to leadership sins, there's perhaps nothing more consistently offensive than failing to do what's been promised. Why? Because when leaders fail to follow through on commitments big or small, people notice, remember, and care when they're let down. Such leaders lose the esteem of their employees, and both morale and productivity suffer.

If you've ever struggled with follow-through, it might help to remember your direct reports are watching and evaluating your ability to honor commitments, which should keep you on your toes! If you tell employees you'll address their concerns about an issue, keep your word, follow up with them, and meet that obligation. After all, you demand the same level of respect and follow-through whenever you ask that of them.

Every commitment you make is a moment of truth—an opportunity to create positive impressions about your leadership abilities and character. The more positive impressions you make, the greater your chances are of winning the trust of those around you. Trust is the seed for growing healthy relationships.

Leverage the following tactics and any others that might support you in this leadership strength:

Define and communicate. When you say you're going to do something, don't just assume you'll remember your promise or obligation. Write it down, set a deadline, and then define and communicate what that follow-up looks like. You want to clue people in on what to expect and when to expect it, as well as who will likely be affected or involved. Use a time management tool to set reminders. Also, send out updates so people know you haven't forgotten or brushed off your commitment.

Don't overcommit. A lot of leaders often say "yes" because they don't know how to say "no." Others overcommit because they're afraid of how it might appear if they don't agree to do something. What they fail to understand, however, is that it's far worse to overpromise and underdeliver than to not commit in the first place. What's more, people actually have respect for leaders who know when to say "no" and can recognize their own limitations.

Get the help you need. Sometimes an activity can look pretty doable, even easy at first. Once you get into the thick of it, however, it becomes more complicated, taking on a life of its own. It's important to have the ability to get additional resources if needed. After all, calling for extra support or assistance to follow through on a commitment can be an effective method for fulfilling a promise or coming through with your end of a deal. Failing to get the necessary help could end up being even more costly in terms of a broken commitment and damaged leadership credibility.

In Summary: The Disciplined Leader honors commitments because doing so is a high-impact activity. How you handle the actions you agreed to take can make or break your entire reputation as a leader—your leadership brand. Do what you say you're going to do, and you'll build respect and credibility.

Take Action!

✓ Create a process to track and follow up with your commitments. Put a verbal commitment in writing and send the proof of that commitment to the other person.

✓ Establish a process of accountability to hold your team members accountable for following up on their commitments.

✓ Learn to say "no" when someone asks you to do something that's not your "Vital Few." If possible and appropriate, explain why you might be turning down the request.

Don't Overuse the "I" Word

You probably know people in your personal or professional life who overuse the "I" word. (Hint: It's that person who is constantly saying, "I did this" or "I did that.") People like this make me smile because they're almost comical. Caught up in their own world, they don't even recognize what they're doing and how annoying and problematic their "I" talk can be. This communication behavior incessantly seeks attention from any and all audiences, solely for the purpose of self-validation—and it's definitely something to avoid as you're developing and practicing your leadership.

A lot of leaders tend to use a lot of "I" talk early on in their careers. They overuse and misuse it because they are immature, aggressive, inexperienced, and trying to get ahead of the pack by promoting themselves and their accomplishments. One of my best bosses once warned me about the dangers of overusing the word "I." That advice became a game changer for how I managed my future communications, particularly in the responsibility to lead my team.

Likewise, when MAP's consultants work with their clients on the topic of communication, this subject often comes up and gets addressed because it's common and needs to be changed. As we tell our clients, your strategy as a leader is to share recognition and focus more on the team than on yourself. Instead of overusing and misusing "I," effective leaders load up their language with "we" words, particularly when communicating about results, accomplishments, and progress—those key elements and outcomes so dependent on teamwork. Saying more of the "We did that" instead of "I did that" in your conversations will consistently demonstrate and reinforce your belief that winning is a team effort, not yours alone. It also serves to recognize and support the contributions of others, building the leadership credibility you'll need to motivate your people and drive results. Here are some specific suggestions around putting this practice into action:

> **Leverage "we" words to build accountability.** Learn to regularly use "we" language to send the message that "we" are equally accountable, meaning you and all the team members either fail together or succeed together. Make yourself less visible in the ownership of successes by assigning the ownership of the results, accomplishments, and progress to the team, such as "Our goals as a team are that we plan to hit $120 million in revenue by year's end and grow our customer base by 10 percent." Aim to give the impression that you've become somewhat lost in the dynamics. For instance, when a football team wins, everyone knows the coach plays a major role. But when it comes time for his interview, what does a good coach do? He immediately deflects any attention on his role in the win and puts the spotlight on the team. A team that gets all the proper props and praise isn't just a great team, but one that will be inspired and motivated to do more of what's right—something that should be every leader's goal.

Know when the "I" word *is* useful. There will be times when it's appropriate and important for you to use more "I" and "me" language. Some examples could include taking a stance on a tough subject, sharing vital perspectives, justifying a position, taking responsibility for a failure, and explaining a new company direction. Good leaders learn when and how to use this good communication style to their advantage. If you're not in the habit of using "I" all the time, when you do speak up about yourself, people will be more likely to listen.

Inspire a culture of "we" people. Just like that great boss I had, you need to pass this lesson on to your team members because your job is to develop them into leaders who can apply this same habit to their teams. "I" employees can actually derail the progress of the team by stealing the credit for group results, accomplishments, and successes. When MAP's consultants coach others on this habit and point out the benefits of focusing on the team instead of themselves, they provide feedback in real time and help them understand how to change their communication approach. They flip words like "I" or "my" to "we" and "our." As a result, the positive impact on their leadership and the people around them is significant, building newfound ownership and a sense of cohesiveness with team projects.

As you adopt this communication behavior, you can also look for opportunities to coach and teach others on how to reflect this mindset. As the tendency to use this type of language becomes more commonplace with you and your people, it will likely become a key aspect of your culture, even an attribute that differentiates you from your competition.

In Summary: The Disciplined Leader understands the power that a "we" mentality has to create an energized, collaborative team and effectively drive results. The "I" mentality is a quick way to diminish loyalty to your leadership brand.

Take Action!

✓ Look for opportunities to give specific recognition for specific accomplishments. Every day select a way to recognize your team using "we."

✓ Learn to recognize yourself privately, but not publicly. Take the word "I" out of your vocabulary when addressing your team. If necessary, have a trusted colleague count the number of times you say "I" in the next five meetings.

✓ Make yourself less visible when it comes to wins. Refrain from taking the credit when your people have worked hard to make success possible or played some role in the achievement.

Surround Yourself with Great Talent

There's no question about it: your ability to lead people starts with you. The reality is your team's performance will ultimately determine the level of your success. Yet many leaders get caught up in mistakenly thinking great leadership is all about their personal talent and abilities. Worse, they sometimes let their insecurities or egos get in the way of working with people who can do things better than they can. Those are the very types of leaders who ultimately fail because today's very best leaders are purposefully and strategically surrounding themselves with talented teams of people. These carefully chosen individuals possess skills and innate gifts that surpass those of their leaders. These employees are working alongside their leaders and behind the scenes, driving productivity, profitability, and overall success.

Part of your responsibility to lead your team requires finding the very best personnel and helping them achieve their full potential. You must also choose those who have the capacity to deliver according to job requirements and exude openness to learning and growth when asked or required.

Over the years, it's been amazing how often leaders have told me their greatest reward has been enabling people to succeed. That has become their legacy. For you, that legacy starts to become possible when you take that first step to surround yourself with the right people. This includes those who have great talent, those you can believe in, those you can trust, and those you really get excited about inspiring because it's simply an extraordinary experience to watch them grow and achieve professionally.

If surrounding yourself with great talent is a crucial component to Disciplined Leadership, then you've got to scrutinize whom you're adding to your team. When you've got the right talent, you must further discipline yourself to find the best ways to motivate these individuals and maximize each and every team member's potential. Here are several key habits around doing just that:

> **Leverage what you've got.** One way to maximize talent is to put your efforts into aligning your employees' strengths to their responsibilities. You'll not only cultivate a happier, more satisfied team but a more loyal, productive one, too, the benefits of which are greater performance, productivity, and, hopefully, revenue and profit.
>
> For example, let's say a sales manager has a business-development employee who excels at working on large opportunities, and the more complex the better. When the manager looks at the numbers, he realizes that this individual outperforms everybody on these prospects. To maximize this employee's strengths, the manager starts assigning him these types of sales opportunities. Almost immediately, sales increase, and the bottom line improves.
>
> In this situation, the manager wisely matched talent to opportunity through a high-performing employee. It's a simple strategy, really, but one that only worked because the manager decided to do it.

He took initiative when he spotted an opportunity, and this became a successful strategy for driving performance, productivity, and results.

Showcase your people's talents. Disciplined Leaders recognize that their role isn't to be perceived as the smartest, most talented person in the business. Nor is it yours. Your responsibility is to look for ways to let your team members shine. As you've learned, everybody is extraordinary and has unique gifts. When you let people apply their skills to work as well as capitalize on their unique gifts, they will perform at an optimum level. They succeed because they are given an environment in which their abilities and talents are valued and recognized.

Provide development opportunities. If you want to surround yourself with great talent, you've got to give your team self-development opportunities. In fact, you should have a dedicated management system for cultivating the potential of your employees' skills and talents, fostering a culture that inspires personal achievement and professional fulfillment. You will lose great employees to other opportunities—that's just a part of business. But when you create a fostering atmosphere like this, people tend to leave less often. Why? Because you're providing growth opportunities and investing in their future.

In Summary: The Disciplined Leader knows the value of assembling great talent, including selecting people who are more knowledgeable on certain subjects than the leader is. Doing so is a key strategy for maximizing team performance, reaching goals, and driving results.

Take Action!

✓ Have a written development plan for your people. Provide opportunities for them to grow and demonstrate their talent.

✓ Conduct regular, scheduled coaching sessions with your people. Give them feedback and suggestions on how they can continue to improve.

✓ Assign people specific responsibilities that challenge them to grow. Look for opportunities to recognize good performance where they're demonstrating their talents.

Hire Who Is Right

Disciplined Leaders clearly understand people are their greatest asset. I've hammered away at this concept. While this principle seems obvious, it can easily be overlooked when you're busy running the daily business and managing a variety of leadership responsibilities. Habitually poor hiring decisions can really prove detrimental to your entire business and undermine your focus on The Vital Few. In fact, your ability to succeed or fail can often be tied to the hires you choose. You may have the best products or services, but without the right team, you will struggle with driving results and achieving goals.

It's quite possible, however, that you've fallen victim to the "warm body syndrome," employing someone simply because he or she had a pulse. When MAP first starts working with its clients on managing people, the "warm body syndrome" often comes up. Many of these leaders admit they've succumbed to rash hiring mistakes, then realized how detrimental it's been to their workplace culture, bottom line, and other precious resources. The true cost of a bad hire can be astronomical, running as high as hundreds of thousands of dollars when you factor in such variables as training, severance pay, mistakes, failures, impact to other employees, missed opportunities, and even lawsuits.

Build a disciplined strategy around consistently holding out for the right person, and you'll reap the rewards that come with a smart hiring decision. Without a doubt, it can feel like the weight of the world is on your shoulders when you're being pressured to fill a hole in your workforce. But remember, it's when you're under such constraints that it's so essential to control impulses, manage any fears, and maintain clarity about your hiring objectives. When you're faced with a vacancy on your team, here's how you can hire smarter:

Start with a job description. One of the best ways to ensure you get the right person is to outline what you truly want with a thorough job description. The job description becomes your roadmap for interviewing candidates and determining if they've got what it takes. For example, if you really need someone with strong teamwork skills but you are interviewing an individual who sounds like the Lone Ranger, this candidate is an unlikely fit. That job description, outlining the desired qualifications, becomes *the* guide for the process.

Don't cave under pressure. Our consultants have often coached managers and leaders who have struggled with hiring because they had the wrong goal. For example, their goal was to fill the position as soon as possible rather than fill the position with the right person. Time trumped quality, which led to a hiring mistake. Then they came across someone else who would have been significantly more qualified. So, too, when internal or external forces are pressuring you to make a speedy hiring decision, and no one currently fits the bill, do your best not be reactive. Pay attention to any red flags when you're interviewing potential candidates. Whether it's an obvious lack of communication skills, a spotty employment history, or a clear inability to fill out the application properly, these and myriad other warning signs shouldn't be ignored.

Understand the impact of a bad hire. In our MAP workshops, we discuss how hiring the wrong people results in spending 80 percent of your time managing these people and the problems that arise. When that happens, the good performers don't get the attention they deserve because you're putting out fires tied to the problematic hires instead. If your company loses a few thousand dollars while you're looking for the perfect person, consider this interesting tidbit: In MAP's experience working with its clients, 80 percent of their company turnover is directly tied to bad hiring decisions. Add that to all the other hard and soft costs of any unfortunate hiring decisions you've made, and you might suddenly be grateful for the short-term pain that can come along with holding out for the right person and securing long-term gain.

In Summary: The Disciplined Leader clearly understands a key responsibility of leadership is attracting the right people to the team. Rush into hiring just to fill a vacancy, and you could end up paying big in lost productivity, poor company morale, and failure to hit goals. If in doubt, don't hire.

Take Action!

✓ As part of your selection process, form a selection committee to ensure you get different perspectives on the candidate.

✓ Develop a comprehensive onboarding plan for the new employee.

✓ Provide "best hiring practices" training for your management team.

Empower Employees

In the world of business leadership, there is so much out there about empowerment or empowering leaders. But do you ever struggle with understanding what those buzzwords really mean, much less how you can become effective at empowering your people?

At MAP, we consistently tell our clients that one of the most effective ways to empower employees is to get them involved in making decisions about the business. There's nothing mysterious or complex here: When you drive decision making down into the organization and give people the freedom to make good business decisions, it becomes a formidable strategy for inspiring others to achieve goals. It communicates that you trust and respect them, which is exactly what your people need. They've got to understand they can make a difference in the organization. Will some mistakes happen? Sure, but the alternative is believing you must come up with all the answers.

The opposite of empowering people is micromanaging them. You probably know exactly what the micromanaging leader looks like. It's the boss who can't let go of whatever task

145

he or she has assigned to others. It's that leader who never trusts that work will get done according to the goals, timelines, and strategies that were set. This person has to get involved in The Vital Few *and* The Trivial Many, control everything to some degree, and take ownership of the outcomes.

It's quite possible you've worked for someone like this. Or, maybe you exude that classic micromanaging behavior yourself. If you have trouble letting go of the details even when you're managing high performers, you're probably struggling in this area—and experiencing problems because of it. For instance, if you're overmanaging competent people, they may grow resentful. We see this dynamic playing out all the time with clients who come to MAP for leadership development. Micromanaging is a common habit with developing leaders, but one that must be broken to release the bonds from The Trivial Many and focus on The Vital Few. Once done, it can be a game changer for empowering people, breathing new life into the workplace culture, and inspiring greater performance and productivity.

Here's how to micromanage less and empower more:

Trust your people. If you want to be an empowering leader, you need to send a message of trust to your team. Don't question the everyday minutia of your people's jobs. Develop them, instead, by letting go of control and inspiring them to take matters into their own hands. Train them if necessary, even if it takes a little more time than you'd like. If you don't, they'll pick up on the fact you really don't believe in them or want to see them excel. Consequently, they'll spend more of their precious time keeping you off their back instead of getting work done. The last thing you want to do is be perceived as a control freak who needs to know everything that's happening every moment of the day. So remember, part of being a Disciplined Leader is trusting your people. This won't just foster employee growth and productivity, but it will also attract the best and brightest to your team.

Know your role. It's impossible to be effective if you're both leading your company and doing the work of others. You have to choose to do one or the other. True, there are situations in which you will have to lead by example and get down in the trenches with those under your command. But do that too often, and you won't lead effectively. In fact, you'll be letting down the people who expect you to remain front and center, set strategies, and keep them focused on goals.

That's exactly what one of MAP's clients discovered when this individual was in a critical juncture of his career as president of his firm. This person loved to do the technical work but had to decide whether he wanted to lead his company or be one of its lead innovators, perhaps finding someone else to serve in his current leadership role. It wasn't until a MAP senior consultant coached him that he realized that he did, indeed, want to lead the company forward in its booming growth. But he had to change his approach and focus on The Vital Few, leaving many technical tasks to his direct reports.

The moral: be careful about getting lost in or sucked into the work of your organization, taking on the types of tasks that really belong to others. Empower your people, assigning more of the right work to the right people. Rather than routinely helping others do their jobs, rely on them to take full ownership, recognize them for their contributions, and inspire them to do more, so you can get back to your responsibilities of focusing on The Vital Few.

Give your frontline employees "the power," as well. All too often, those working on the front lines of customer service aren't allowed to make decisions on their own. They're forbidden to take action with the customers they interact with daily. True, you need certain policies and procedures to keep business running efficiently and profitably, but it can be far more productive to give that frontline team the authority to make decisions about customer issues or problems within certain parameters.

In Summary: The Disciplined Leader intuitively understands the concept of team and individual empowerment. If you truly want to join the ranks of Disciplined Leaders, send the message that you trust and value your team. The higher morale and employee growth will spur and sustain productivity and enable you to focus on your Vital Few.

Take Action!

✓ Define the benefits you will receive if you become better at empowering your employees.

✓ Evaluate how well you are doing with empowering your people. Take corrective action to address any gaps.

✓ Develop your coaching skills to become more effective at empowering your employees.

Hold Your Team Accountable

For our clients, MAP defines accountability as measuring performance and taking timely, appropriate action—and it's a common source of angst and challenge for many of them. For example, since 1960, MAP has worked with tens of thousands of business leaders and entrepreneurs, most of whom have wrestled with challenges tied to accountability. Leaders struggle with holding their teams and organizations accountable, creating a host of problems that suck time and energy away from their Vital Few.

Why? There are a lot of reasons and excuses around why accountability never gets implemented. Some of these clients lack confidence and experience in accountability leadership. Others confide they're frustrated with poor performance from employees, yet they haven't established an accountability system for driving performance. Regardless of why they're having trouble, we always tell them sustainable results and success depend upon how effective these leaders are at executing around accountability. Fail to hold people accountable, and results will suffer.

Any business in any industry can suffer at the expense of poor accountability. But in family-owned businesses, lack of accountability is often prolific. One particular MAP client upheld a corporate culture in which all the owners and employees were either family members or friends of the family, and they were all implementing the "hope strategy." Everyone just *hoped* everyone else would do their jobs and *hoped* this strategy would deliver companywide peace and profitability. But they were not meeting their goals, and no one, most of all the key family leaders, was genuinely happy about this fact.

At one particular pain point, the family leaders started working with one of our senior consultants to implement MAP's system for accountability. With this method, the vice president of sales started setting just three measurable, monthly goals. In a very short timeframe, however, it became clear that setting these measurable, timely goals made a positive difference. So the company leadership expanded the system to the entire sales team of ten. Collectively, the sales force now had thirty monthly, measurable goals. It turned out that most people liked being held accountable. Meeting measurable goals or taking corrective action against missed targets felt like progress. The progress became downright inspiring for an organization of people who wanted to excel and, ironically, were now filled with *real* hope.

That said, not everyone in the family business survived this transformation. Some people couldn't deal with the change and expectations and either resigned or were terminated. But keeping the interest of the company a priority, the accountability system took the personality and politics out of the equation, significantly influencing and supporting those who remained.

Given this story, think about the accountability levels on your team and within your organization. How would you rate accountability—poor, fair, or good? Does it need some attention from you? If so, address it. But one word of caution: real accountability requires sheer discipline if it is going to work. It's not easy, but the effort and short-lived pain are worth the gain. In fact, this discipline is essential for you to be an effective accountability leader. Here are three ways to execute against accountability:

Establish an accountability system. It's really tough for an accountability leader to operate solo. If you want to be an accountability leader, you must drive the accountability down into the organization to fully impact your organization. The best method is with a proven system that gets every team member on the same page and focused on the right measures. The system you choose must tap the power of putting performance measurements in place and monitoring those numbers. At MAP, we call these measures Vital Factors, the key indicators of a team's performance. We implement Vital Factor meetings with clients to create a needed accountability system. These meetings also provide insight around what's working and what isn't, who needs coaching, and, ultimately, who is engaged and not engaged. Whether you use a system like MAP's or put an alternative solution in place, having such a structure is essential for effectively monitoring, measuring, and addressing performance.

Take corrective action when necessary. One of your responsibilities as an accountability leader is coaching your team to take corrective action against missed goals. This isn't about "being tough" or "authoritarian" but rather reinforcing the importance of hitting goals. When you coach a direct report to develop corrective actions against missed goals, that individual will own the problem and become accountable to it. If you have individuals who consistently miss their goals, consider coaching. The coaching will be more effective when you've got measurements in place.

Recognize good performance. Recognizing and rewarding good performance is the upside to developing and achieving accountability. It's the payoff for measuring and highlighting peak performance. Determine the best ways to motivate your people as teams and individuals, taking into account studies that show people aren't always motivated by rewards that are external in nature, such as money. In fact, *Harvard Business Review* shows that "employees who are intrinsically motivated are three times more engaged than employees who are extrinsically motivated"[7] by such things as money and other tangibles.

Want to build that engagement? Then focus more on your people's achievements, motivate them to want to succeed, and help them experience the value of an accountability system in that way. Recognize good performance. Be specific about what they accomplished, providing examples and metrics so the recognition has more impact. Avoid just saying, "You did a good job." A better approach to praise could be: "You worked without a single error for the last month—that's a record at our company."

In Summary: The Disciplined Leader values accountability as the benchmark for measuring performance and taking appropriate, timely action. People are genuinely motivated by accountability; they value feedback and the discipline of deadlines. Consistently hold your team accountable to drive goal achievement and overall results.

Take Action!

✓ Evaluate your accountability leadership and develop actions that will make you more effective at holding people accountable.

✓ Implement monthly accountability meetings, making sure there are no other items on the agenda other than reviewing performance against goals and developing corrective actions.

✓ Coach your team to quickly develop corrective actions when they miss goals to create immediate ownership and timely accountability.

Check up Daily on Goals

You now know why holding your people accountable through an accountability system that includes corrective actions and performance recognition is so important to your organization's success. Now let's dig deeper into the topic of leveraging daily accountability. Specifically, we're going to delve into what you can regularly do to reinforce your commitment to accountability and build more discipline around managing performance.

For starters, you want to adopt a "driving" management style and develop tactics that align with this approach. This practice will communicate the importance of managing performance daily, not just whenever your people gather for the next team meeting. Also, don't just ask your employees how things are going in general—you'll probably get a black-and-white answer or some watered-down version of reality. Instead, ask them how they are performing against their goals, what they need to do next, and why they are struggling. Pose the tough questions and don't necessarily let them off easy when they answer. Ensure this conversation becomes an opportunity to coach and motivate them, making this one of your daily habits.

A common trait with Disciplined Leaders who are really great at driving results is they are goal-minded. They start their day thinking about where people are in relationship to their goals and how they're doing in terms of performance. These leaders allocate a percentage of their time to measure, assess, and address this performance day in and day out. This regular check-in keeps people on their toes, builds transparency around where everyone is at, and drives people to perform. Such check-ins are short in nature, professional, and efficient—free of any diversions or fluffy conversation that could derail the intentions behind the check-in.

Here are three more solid ways to manage performance daily:

Implement flash reporting. Information is powerful, particularly when it comes to developing effective ways to monitor and report your team's performance daily. One way to do all this can be through "flash reporting"—a method for communicating results in relationship to established goals.

For instance, many of our clients develop systems and processes that give them vital results through a daily "dashboard" instead of waiting for month-end reports. It could be as simple as providing the information in an Excel spreadsheet or through a software application that's designed just for this purpose. Whatever tool is used for flash reporting, this tactic delivers a chance to see what's going on, reinforces what's going right, and allows for more timely corrective actions. It's an easy way to sharpen everyone's daily focus by communicating about performance in relationship to goals.

Manage by walking around. Really want to know what's going on with your team and how they're performing? Get out of your office, stroll around the workplace, and get the information you need. Find out what's really happening, asking your employees insightful, probing questions like, "How are you doing in relationship to your goals?" "What challenges are you having—and why?" "Why are customers responding to us in the way you just described?" Just asking "How's it going?" isn't enough. Get your people's thoughts on why things are happening, what improvements need to be made, and how to ensure that the best corrective actions are taken.

Implement "daily huddles." Some years ago, I witnessed the impact of daily huddles when I worked for a Fortune 500 company. Every morning, we would have a short meeting with teams of frontline employees to discuss the results from the previous day's goals and establish goals for the current day. This tactic created razor-sharp focus on performance. Consequently, across-the-board customer service levels dramatically increased.

This practice also worked wonders for a manager who was later asked to turn around a business unit for the same company. He called a team huddle every morning to create a sense of urgency, inspire everyone with his positive attitude, and reinforce a commitment to the goal. So, too, a team huddle can help you increase your people's focus on what's vital and motivate them to perform in greater alignment with their goals.

In Summary: The Disciplined Leader understands the value of a daily performance review and how it can maximize the impact of leadership, improve accountability, and sustain the overall strategy. Your consistent efforts to create team focus on your Vital Few can drive greater performance, accelerate goal achievement, and deliver results faster.

Take Action!

✓ Challenge yourself to spend fifteen minutes a day to manage by walking around. Ask employees insightful, probing questions that focus on performance and the problems they are facing.

✓ Hold a one-to-one meeting with your direct reports. Communicate your expectations around how they should regularly report performance to you.

✓ At your next team meeting, evaluate your performance reporting and process. Determine how to report results more in real time and assign the right person to oversee this project.

Give Effective Performance Feedback

Have you ever sat down with a boss for your annual review and been blasted for something that you didn't do right—but months ago? If so, how did you feel? Confused? Angry? Even a little "set up" or deceived? Probably so, because receiving feedback (particularly the negative kind) on performance that happened long ago is like having someone throw you a curveball. You can't see it coming, and it's challenging to manage with grace because the feedback is a total surprise.

If you have a leadership position today, you're the one sitting in the boss's seat. As such, the tables are turned. It's now your responsibility to deliver annual performance reviews to your staff. The onus is on you to carefully consider how you're giving feedback to your team. For instance, are you delivering regular communications to individuals about their performance, or do you tend to put this activity off or forget about it until the annual performance review arrives? If you're doing either of these things, it's time to change your approach. It may take some effort up front, but delivering frequent feedback can make you and your team more effective.

One of MAP's top clients had a sales director who gave lackluster sales presentations. Although this team leader delivered solid results, he displayed no enthusiasm—no fire in his belly—when it came to reporting results and inspiring others on the sales team. The CEO thought this sales director needed to be terminated, but MAP's consultant cautioned against it. He suggested performance feedback, specifically coaching this individual to improve upon his presentation delivery and amplify his impact on others. The CEO took the advice, and it worked.

Some aspects of people are coachable; others are not. This was one of those areas in which someone could be coached for improvement. In the end, it made a great difference not just in the sales director's presentation delivery but his ability to inspire his audiences, including his boss, the sales team, key company stakeholders, and others.

Performance feedback also gives you an opportunity to focus more often on what the employee is doing right, which is proven to be a far greater motivator than harping on wrongs or weaknesses. If you're spending more time addressing an employee's shortcomings or failures, you need to determine if you've got the right hire in the first place or whether you're simply not aligning that employee's strengths and skills to the right position or responsibilities.

Ultimately, regular feedback is a communication tool that creates transparency in the workplace and improves results. Why is that so important? Because transparency breeds loyalty, and loyalty plays a big role in increasing productivity and goal achievement. And that, no doubt, directly supports your Vital Few.

If you want to make feedback effective, here is what I suggest:

Be quick about it. There's nothing more powerful than giving real-time feedback on performance right after you witness an action. This is a high-impact activity because whatever just took place is fresh in the employee's mind. The sooner you provide feedback, the less defensive the person will be because there's no time delay during which aspects of what happened can be forgotten. The person receiving this feedback will be more receptive because you can be a lot more descriptive based upon what you just witnessed.

Coach, don't tell. It never pays to just tell someone that you expect change. You need to help them understand the issue and coach them around the solutions. Setting up regular coaching sessions can provide an ideal platform for giving feedback on performance and coaching for improvement. To establish accountability, guide your employees in developing their own corrective actions and make sure they commit to some type of timeframe for improvement.

It's important to use the word "coaching session" when you set up the meeting with an employee, too. A "coaching session" doesn't sound punitive. It's more supportive, even collaborative in nature. After all, these one-on-one meetings are about helping the individual improve in areas in which they may be struggling. Make sure to use an effective, nonthreatening coaching style and pick the right time and place for these sessions.

Use accountability meetings. As you learned earlier, an accountability meeting is a great tool for getting your team focused on performance. If you're in a meeting with your direct reports and they are reporting progress against their goals, this is another opportunity to provide timely feedback and revisit expectations. Make sure you use the right communication style. "You screwed up, Larry," doesn't exactly open lines of communication. Neither does, "Rosina, you don't know what you're doing." That's attacking the person instead of attacking the problem, which is the opposite of what you want to do. So think "supportive," and encourage other team members to help by giving their suggestions and sharing experiences that will further empower others to overcome their challenges.

In Summary: The Disciplined Leader understands the power of immediate feedback as well as the dangers and lost opportunities of delayed feedback. Coach others on their performance through one-on-one coaching sessions and accountability meetings to help them develop and grow.

Take Action!

✓ Schedule regular coaching sessions with your team members to focus on their development and performance.

✓ Have a monthly accountability system where you review monthly performance and give feedback.

✓ Make sure you're being equitable about giving feedback to everyone. Don't just concentrate on poor performers but on good performers, too.

Spot Opportunities to Coach

Most leaders want to fix problems. They usually enjoy sharing knowledge and ideas to help their team improve and achieve goals. Telling employees how to do their jobs correctly is necessary in some situations. However, it is also important to recognize teachable moments with your team in which asking them good questions and encouraging them to come up with the answers becomes the far more effective approach. Why? When they find the answers to their own problems, it will become a richer, more meaningful learning experience. Developing your staff through coaching opportunities can reap the kinds of rewards that make a more lasting, sustainable difference. It's a strategy that will empower your people with sharper skills, new strengths, and greater overall confidence in their jobs.

At MAP, one of the qualities we seek when we hire consultants is their ability to coach clients effectively. The last thing our clients want is to be told what to do all the time by their consultant. What they really want—and need—is someone to provide solid tools and expertise but then guide them around how to leverage what they're learning to accelerate their performance. While that's something they get through their coaching, they invariably pick up on how they can be more effective at their own coaching and how influential that approach can be on their people. When they, in turn, coach their employees, they see greater results in goal achievement, morale, and success overall.

To maximize the productivity and performance of your team, you need to become a great coach. While telling your employees how to do something might seem like the fastest, easiest way to develop them, it's not the best approach. Coaching takes time and self-discipline on your part, but it's more effective in terms of getting the changes and results you need. Stay the course with this strategy to help your people excel and take your leadership to that next level.

Here are three examples of opportunities—or teachable moments—in which it definitely pays to coach:

When a team member is missing goals. You may well know why Ted, one of your direct reports, is not achieving his number-one goal. But if you tell him why, he might simply hear the reason without understanding its root cause. And the root cause is what you're after because that's what he will need to understand and address through corrective action. The best way to instill that understanding and help him get to the heart of the matter is through discovery questions. Instead of inquiring about "what" happened, ask Ted why he failed to achieve his goals. This should start a more meaningful discussion. The more "whys" you ask, the deeper he will have to dig, and the closer he will get to the real problem.

When a team member is struggling with relationships. Business is all about people, yet it's a fact of life that certain people struggle with relationships. The inability to get along with others is a common career derailer for people, so it's important to address this behavior if you're seeing it among your team.

If you recognize that Amy doesn't get along with her coworkers and is seriously lacking some people skills, take action. Set aside time to coach her for improvement because it is critical to her relationships and overall success. Ask "Why?" questions to determine if there's a root cause to the friction. Help her determine on her own how well she has managed the conflict thus far. Then share insights based upon your own experiences. Coaching team members to manage their relationships successfully is worth the effort. Tackling this common issue with a conscientious coaching approach can turn a losing situation into a win-win for all.

When a team member is needing a solution. Certain individuals on your team may sometimes hit a wall and not know what to do. For example, say one of your direct reports, Maria, has a habit of running to you, hoping to get quick solutions to her problems. While it's a common tendency to want to help people, resist the temptation to let this tendency become a habit. If you repeat this behavior over and over, you will be enabling Maria to depend upon you to solve all her challenges. Becoming her "answer guru" is the last thing you want to transpire. If you're faced with this type of situation, slow down and ask your employees to find their own solutions by asking those critical "Why?" questions.

In Summary: The Disciplined Leader must be a great coach, although this doesn't necessarily come naturally to everyone. As you manage your team, incorporate coaching as one of your primary leadership styles. Learn to recognize opportunities to coach and make an impact.

Take Action!

✓ Develop your coaching skills; never assume you know how to coach. Look for specific training opportunities to develop your coaching skills, such as certificate programs and other credentialed organizations.

✓ Find a proven coaching model and adopt a structured coaching process that works for you. Practice the model you've adopted and make adjustments to refine it.

✓ Get a coach for yourself. Use the process to help develop your personal coaching skills.

#35

Demand More Solutions

When I was a young supervisor, I really didn't understand leadership to any significant degree. I worked my way up through the company thanks to hard work and teamwork. After my first promotion, I remember sitting in my office and suddenly thinking, "What am I supposed to be doing?" This particular company didn't offer any type of management or leadership training, so I was left to my own devices to form the model of how to manage and lead. As a part of that model, I made a concerted effort to provide solutions to my team whenever anyone came to me in need of an answer or help. I thought this was the epitome of leadership.

Big mistake. My office quickly became a revolving door for everyone and anyone who had a problem. It took me a while to figure it out, but this was anything but a solution to my leadership challenges, particularly in relationship to my responsibility to lead my team.

So do you find yourself being the "answer guru" for all problems big and small? Is there a perpetual line of employees streaming in and out of your office, looking to you to handle all their problems? If so, that's a pretty good indicator that you're probably guilty of spending too much time providing all the answers, which is a leadership habit that has been linked to stunted employee growth, among many other things.

Avoid this pitfall, making a commitment to stop this habit. Instead of providing everyone with easy directives and solutions, create a new rule: for every problem your employees bring you, demand that they come armed with two potential solutions. Follow this approach, and you'll notice the following benefits. First, it will eliminate that traffic line outside your office. Second, it can accelerate the professional development and capacity of your people. When you release unnecessary control and inspire your people to take matters into their control, you will essentially turn these codependent problem communicators into independent problem solvers. This strategy, which builds upon your vital leadership goal to empower your employees, will better equip your staff members to manage their own solutions and learn more about themselves and the business along the way.

Here are some tips to support that process:

Provide guidance. You're not going to wave some magic wand and suddenly create adept problem solvers. Your staff members are going to be uncomfortable and lack confidence with problem solving if you don't provide coaching and guidance first. Therefore, coach them on how to tap into the power of team consulting and leverage their peers or other employees who might have the wisdom and experience to help them develop solutions. When they reach out to people, they will likely find there are always good team members who care and will collaborate to help. They can also use outside resources, everything from books, webinars, and how-to articles on particular topics or business challenges to more formal education methods such as training, workshops, seminars, and professional courses.

Reinforce success. Since people won't transform into problem solvers overnight, you need to work on recognizing achievements of all sizes. When success happens, whether it is big or small, that becomes the perfect opportunity to reinforce the behavior, so publicly recognize those victories and communicate the wins. Reinforcing what those on your team are doing right will have the biggest impact. In terms of your role, you'll find that you've become someone who monitors and sustains success as opposed to being the primary problem solver in your group. Consistently reinforcing the right behaviors will slowly reshape the attitudes and abilities around problem solving, building greater efficiencies and morale.

Resist the urge to trump someone's good idea. Even if you believe your approach is the best, sometimes embracing a direct report's mediocre solution can be more effective than your "better solution." Particularly if the matter is not urgent or critical to the company's health or viability, roll with some of the solutions just to see where they go and give your direct report an opportunity to see his or her solution in the works. This is a coaching technique, not unlike when a coach lets the quarterback on a football team go ahead with a certain play. Regardless of whether you think a particular solution will work, one thing is for sure: you will truly never know unless you give your team member the "green light" to run that particular play.

In Summary: The Disciplined Leader demands a continuum of solutions. Demanding more solutions is a discipline that's often challenging for leaders to embrace and follow. Yet the payoff can be huge in terms of how well you can develop decision making among your team and lighten the burdens that come with finding answers for everyone who is not yet a Disciplined Leader.

Take Action!

✓ Make a statement in your next staff meeting to communicate how you're going to address problem solving. Communicate that you will demand more solutions—and why that's important to your personal time and their growth.

✓ For every problem that's brought to you, require two solutions and recommendations related to those solutions, such as implementation, execution, resources, and so on.

✓ Identify individuals or "repeat offenders" who always communicate problems. Provide coaching around problem solving and determine if there's a resource, such as a training program, that will promote their growth.

Encourage Disagreement

If the topic of this lesson makes you a little uncomfortable, I'm not surprised. Over the years, MAP has found this particular bit of advice has never been easy for most to embrace. But to develop the best solutions and outcomes in business, you need to be the kind of leader who encourages disagreement from your team. I'm not talking about asking those individuals to disagree on every whim. But you want them to speak up when they do not agree on important matters, specifically when healthy, constructive dialogue with opposing viewpoints can lead to discovery and, eventually, growth and productivity. Done right, this can foster a high-energy yet professional environment that's rich in creativity, one in which individuals are encouraged and challenged to contribute ideas and solutions.

It's quite possible you've worked in places in which there was too much agreement going on. Such cultures are generally managed by leaders who are uncomfortable with opposing perspectives and don't know how to handle conflicting opinions and ideas with forward-thinking purpose. It's sometimes indicative of leadership immaturity. It can also be a sign of leadership weakness, particularly in relationship to managing the team. Regardless of the reason, the "yes-person" culture shuts down and blocks critical thinking, resulting in poor decision making and missed opportunities. Meanwhile, healthy work cultures demand disagreement, which creates viable possibilities for ingenuity, change, and progress. As a leader, your job is to sponsor this latter type of culture, leading by example. You can do that by following a few guidelines:

Establish ways to make disagreeing "safe." Having worked in both cultures of disagreement and agreement, I've learned that leaders have to make their team members feel free to disagree. This can sometimes be tricky, particularly in organizations that have that traditional top-down style of management. In all levels of your organization, sponsor and initiate a process for constructive disagreement, inviting people to have candid conversations about important issues at hand. Encourage debate and robust communications while moderating any potential aggression or verbal abuse.

Pipe down and pick your battles. Part of making it safe for people to disagree is not being quite so vocal yourself. Don't go to the mat against each and every thing. Take a break to listen to the viewpoints of others, encouraging productive discussion by asking open-ended questions of those around you. The conclusion to the debate might eventually support your perspective or idea. If it doesn't, it might deliver a better idea than you ever previously considered. Speak up when it's truly important, of course, but remember that people will listen to and respect your ideas more if you don't always dominate the discussions.

Learn effective disagreement strategies. This is about the style of your approach and your verbal and nonverbal skills. Are you shaking your head, interrupting, speaking in a raised voice, or, even worse, shouting? Obviously, you want to quit any or all those bad habits and institute some nondefensive communication that opens the door for effective disagreement. For example, don't say, "You're wrong"; say "I see it differently." This simple wordplay will suck out potential, negative energy that's possibly building in the conversation. It's also less personal and emotional, yet more collaborative and factual. Just focus on the problem, not the person. Doing so will diffuse any potential conversation bomb and sustain a neutral ground that breeds healthy debate and differing views.

In Summary: The Disciplined Leader is comfortable with opposition and debate, knowing full well the result is sharper analysis and well-crafted ideas. Your sponsorship of this practice is key to creating a healthy workforce culture in which it is safe to debate for the purpose of generating creative thoughts and solid solutions.

Take Action!

✓ Develop meeting ground rules that sponsor constructive discussion on opposing views.

✓ Practice asking open-ended questions when participating in your next meeting to see if you can draw out opposing views.

✓ Pose a weak idea, argument, or product concept at your next team meeting. See how long it takes before someone (or everyone) shoots you down. If you suspect you have a "yes culture," this is a good test to find out.

Advocate for Your Team

There are times in business when you need to "go to bat" for your team. It is leadership's responsibility to provide support to its team members when tough challenges arise that they can't solve on their own. Whether your team needs resources, training, or other types of support, it is your responsibility to take action that empowers the team to do its job. These situations are great opportunities to show your team members they are your number-one priority. As you demonstrate you have their best interests at heart, your commitment will build respect and loyalty from your team.

At one point in my past, I worked for a boss who did not demonstrate support when it was needed most. This frustrating experience zapped our team's energy and hurt morale. It affected my confidence to make things happen because I didn't feel supported. It was also tough because I felt I was on my own, without backup. Perhaps you have worked for a boss who disengaged from you and other team members in a similar way. If so, you probably experienced some of the same frustrations because it's hard to respect such a complacent leader.

Disciplined Leaders are heavily engaged with their team. For example, it was quite a shock when one of MAP's clients learned the quality of the equipment his team was selling to municipalities was so poor that a major city was returning several of the products, each of which cost about $500,000. So in defense of his sales team, the entire organization, and the customer, the leader worked with MAP to create a plan to challenge the manufacturer to address the quality-control issues. Everyone in the company was on pins and needles when the leader flew to Chicago to stand up to this manufacturer and resolve the problem—but he succeeded with that specific plan in hand. Perhaps most importantly, he sent a message to his organization (and customer) that he was their number-one advocate and would never ask them to sell or do something they couldn't believe in or trust.

There are times when you'll really need to step in and provide that support, too. Here are three prime examples:

Overcoming obstacles. Whether your team members are running the daily operations of the business or are involved in a specific initiative, they will face obstacles they cannot solve on their own. These could include an unforeseen crisis, external competition, or problems with another department in your company. View these as opportunities to demonstrate your commitment to your people. Support them and remove these roadblocks, keeping in mind that everyone on the team is paying attention to your actions when these challenges occur. Avoid complacency at all costs and do what is right, and you will win their respect and secure greater loyalty.

Dealing with unfair criticism. There are times in leadership when you will need to defend a direct report or the entire team. When criticism falls on your team, start by gathering the facts. Gathering the facts will better position you to understand what is behind the criticism and how to respond appropriately. If the criticism is truly unfair and needs to be addressed, take action. Remain professional in your defense, but send a clear message that unfairly criticizing your team is not acceptable. Be cautious not to overadvocate for your team. A fine line exists between defending your team and being defensive.

Providing recognition. A powerful way to advocate for your team is by making sure they get the recognition they deserve. There's nothing that can dampen morale more quickly than when your people think they're being taken for granted because nobody is recognizing their efforts. A culture in which they're recognized for their progress and contribution to the team makes them feel appreciated and motivated. Considering this, your job is to be an avid promoter of your team, the kind of leader who is proud of your people—someone who will stick with and support them through thick and thin. Look for opportunities and successes where you can highlight the team as a whole and make sure everyone on it gets the recognition they deserve.

In Summary: The Disciplined Leader understands that commanding trust and respect among team members means being a strong advocate for the team when resources or other problems arise. Your actions, such as speaking up to others, build a positive work environment and send a strong message that your team is important.

Take Action!

✓ Assess your current effectiveness as an advocate
for your team. Identify any gaps and develop
corrective actions.

✓ Determine the current challenges your team
is facing to get its job done. Get everyone
involved and ask them to identify barriers to
their success or threats to the business.

✓ Look for opportunities to advocate for your
team through recognition. Make sure your team
members get the credit they deserve to build
morale and drive results.

Recognize Your Employees

You now know there's a big myth out there in the business world that money is the top motivator for employees. But as you've also learned, people come to work because they want to feel appreciated, accountable, and productive. That's exactly what MAP has found with motivating individuals. Most people want to do a good job and feel like they're making a difference. Effectively recognizing people for their contributions is a huge motivator.

The trick is to do it right, and it's usually not as easy as simply saying "good job." I've worked with a lot of people who have communication needs that require specificity before any praise helps them. In fact, if I'm too general with people who have this communication style, they become skeptical about my intent to recognize them. For example, it's not as meaningful to say "Way to go on your presentation today" as it would be to say "The energy you displayed really communicated passion and emphasized just how important this project is for us all. It was easy to follow, and your enthusiasm engaged everybody."

This is the type of verbal praise that doesn't just feel good but serves to reinforce what was done right. Your team members can sink their teeth into it. It's not just nice information but useful information because the employee now knows how to meet or even exceed future expectations. Specific praise, given verbally or otherwise, reinforces the behavior while non-specific praise overdone or carelessly misused can amount to being mere flattery.

If you ever find yourself repeatedly saying "good job" like a one-trick pony, try some new tactics for employee recognition. Investing a little thought into how you go about acknowledging and appreciating hard work can have a big impact.

While verbal praise can be highly effective in some situations and for some people, it's not always the most effective way to motivate others. Increased responsibility, advancement, and growth rank among the top-five most powerful motivators.[8] The more effort you put forth, the more it shows you understand your people, really know who they are, and truly value their hard work and contributions to your organization's success.

Here, I've expanded on how to make your employee-appreciation efforts more effective.

Understand an individual's motivators. For example, Brendon might be looking for advancement and growth because it's important to him to feel as if he's moving ahead, not stagnating. And money doesn't motivate Katie—she simply wants to know she's producing quality work and making a difference. Meanwhile, Mark might feel more valued if he was able to apply his skills to an exciting high-profile project. The best way to figure out what truly motivates your people is to know them well enough as individuals to determine the answer. Once you understand your people, you can recognize them with the right reward. When the opportunity presents itself, you'll be able to match their personal motivators to the recognition you provide. So in addition to, or in place of, verbal praise, consider increased responsibilities, promotions, and other growth opportunities to inspire your people's performance.

Be fair. If you don't spread the love around to everyone on your team, your efforts in employee recognition can backfire. For example, say your team successfully completed a project and you singled out a few individuals for their contribution to the success at a luncheon. But you mistakenly overlooked one of the key contributors so that person felt slighted and upset. You just turned a positive into a negative, putting you in damage-control mode. Remember, recognition, while it might seem easy, is a strategy. Be thoughtful about those you acknowledge on your team and how you're recognizing them.

Match recognition to performance. Make sure that the reward matches the contribution. If you give a large bonus for something that truly didn't warrant a large bonus, you're setting yourself up for future trouble because you've set unrealistic expectations. Then again, if you give someone a $20 gift card as a reward for pioneering a solution that saved your company $50,000, you'll cause issues because that person will feel underappreciated.

In Summary: The Disciplined Leader knows how to motivate employees by understanding their intrinsic values and matching their contributions to those values. You've got to be effective in appreciating employees for their contributions. Commit to being specific, matching the right motivators to the individual and taking a balanced approach toward appreciation.

Take Action!

✓ Ask your employees what motivates them. Find ways to align what motivates them to upcoming opportunities, such as new assignments, responsibilities, or projects.

✓ Practice making your praise specific for your staff members. Give details about what was done right.

✓ Recognize your current habits on giving recognition and take corrective actions if necessary.

Wrap-up

MAP helps business leaders engage and align their teams to create breakthrough results. Since 1960, it's simply been what we do best, the critical value we provide through our consulting services for our clients. Now it's your turn to get solid clarity on what aspects of this core area of your leadership responsibility you need to address.

To recap, let's talk about the key points in this past part. We started out with tips focused on how to build engagement and credibility with your team. We then shifted gears a bit to move into advice on developing a performance-based team by hiring the right talent, communicating effectively, and building alignment through timely accountability. Toward the end, you got some coaching about how to inspire performance and get results. You also learned habits to provide effective feedback, recognition, and rewards that demonstrate your commitment to team members.

Take a few minutes to reflect on these subjects. If you need to, flip back through Part II to revisit the topics. What's jumping out at you—which tips are most compelling? Use these prompts to choose your "Top Three" Vital Few. Record those on your *Vital Few Template* on pages 7–8. Once you've got your Vital Few selected here, move on to Part III.

Part III

Extend Your Reach

The Responsibility to Lead Your Organization

This book would be incomplete if I didn't dedicate a portion of it to the responsibility you have to lead your organization. It's the third and final area within the three core areas of your leadership responsibilities—this one rounding out your work from leading yourself and leading your team. Because no leadership journey is ever complete, it also gives our path a temporary resting point.

Here, you can see how the work that's being done on leading yourself and leading the team fortify your total leadership capacity, positioning it for even greater influence through leading your organization. You can also glance at some of the chapter headlines to see how this third part complements the other two.

Leading your organization is about extending your leadership reach beyond yourself and your team to a degree that's much further from you yet still critically connected to your organization's center: you. Among many things, this includes growing your impact on the organization through key mindsets, strategic practices, and supportive habits you adopt, implement, and execute. That's why you'll find that these specific tips are all about boosting your leadership impact by engaging and aligning people organization-wide, carving out and keeping the company's crucial competitive edge, as well as building loyal relationships with the people with whom you do business, your customers. Some of the other tips explore how to create alignment around your vision, accelerate performance through a culture of accountability, nurture an innovative workforce, and build your overall brand into something people trust.

Winning such trust is no doubt a sizeable task in and of itself, and it's one that cannot be accomplished unless there's alignment in your organization—alignment of values and people. When this exists, it results in an effective, empowered organization of people who, led by you, believe in their organization enough to do their jobs well and build relationships with the customers who will support it.

Keep on course with your journey to become a Disciplined Leader, but now accelerate influence and expand your reach. Secure these strategies and support your responsibility to lead your organization, taking on these proven habits and practices.

Develop a "What's the Goal?" Culture

Solid logic suggests placing this lesson first in this current part of the book. Why? Because individuals, teams, and organizations that consistently ask "What's the goal?" are more efficient and goal-oriented. Answer that vital question, and you'll quickly get ahead in any game. It's a way to create definition around objectives, as well as sharpen focus on strategies. At MAP, asking "What's the goal?" is one of the first habits we always coach our clients to adopt. When we start working with a new client, we talk about why it's crucial to our collaboration and how it supports sustainable success. It's essential to good leadership, a best practice for management, and a proven tactic for generating more results for your organization.

Even some of the most seasoned, experienced businesses have learned critical lessons around the importance of understanding "What's the goal?" in all they say and do. For example, the leadership within a seventy-five-year-old business sought out MAP's help after running into some challenges they just couldn't overcome on their own. Up until that point, the business had been successful in spite of itself.

But as soon as MAP coached these leaders around adopting that strategic, "What's the goal?" mindset, things immediately turned around. In fact, in less than a year's time, the company made major changes—all rooted in that "goal" mindset—and revenue jumped 20 percent.

Disciplined Leaders consistently ask "What's the goal?" in both their personal and professional lives—and that's exactly what I'm encouraging you to do, too. For example, when you take on a new activity such as hiking, your goal may be tangible, such as the mountaintop you intend to summit. Or, it could be less tangible, such as maintaining a healthy work-life balance. Likewise, on the professional front, you've got to define those goals. For instance, you've clearly decided to read this very book, but have you determined a specific goal tied to this activity? Perhaps your objective is growing as a leader so you're well positioned for an upcoming promotion. Or maybe it's getting a better grip on managing a specific leadership responsibility within your organization. Whatever your goal is, taking the time to specify it will provide clarity, give you direction, and keep you focused.

Everybody loves guarantees in life. The one thing I guarantee is you're going to save significant time if you drive the "What's the goal?" habit in your company. For example, you've probably watched your team invest copious hours on an assignment only to learn later the work turned out to be unusable. It happens a lot in business. Without clearly defined goals, people in organizations squander time and other resources working on activities that don't really matter—or aren't vital, as we say at MAP. The lack of clearly defined goals for work activities results in inefficiency and poor execution. So start a practice of asking "What's the goal?" in your organization, carefully considering the following strategies:

> **Always set goals for meetings.** How many meetings have you attended that were a big waste because people just sat around having nice discussions and no conclusions or agreements were made? If you're having

a meeting just to have it, you might as well cancel it. Let everyone keep on working. Having a meeting without a goal and an agenda is sort of like telling people to show up for a race with no finish line. It's pointless. Yet how many meetings have you sat in on and wondered, "Why the heck am I here?" MAP always recommends defining the meeting's goals when planning the agenda. This discipline will keep the agenda items more focused and aligned to whatever you want to accomplish. Equally important, the meeting leader should kick it off by communicating the objectives to everyone. This person should state the goals, making sure they are specific, clearly spoken, easy to grasp, and well understood. For example, "In today's meeting, I'd like to accomplish x, y, and z within our two-hour time frame. Does everyone understand our goals?"

Build in goals with every project. If someone is assigned a new responsibility or project, it's equally important to set the stage for success by using the "What's the goal?" approach. If you don't, you may miss the mark because the deliverable might not meet others' expectations.

In one of my previous professional roles, I was asked to manage companywide projects. As part of my responsibility, I had to work cross-functionally and provide progress updates to the senior team. It didn't take me long to realize this team was not at all aligned to its project goals, and this fact made my life miserable because I had to keep making course corrections. Eventually, however, I learned to get all the team members in a room just to define and document both the goals of the project and their expected outcomes. This activity paid off in a big way. The understanding and consensus around the right goals eliminated the need for me to run interference and troubleshoot problems later.

Define your goals before starting anything. Your day is undoubtedly filled with lots of planned and un-planned action items. As you learned in Part II of the book, one of the best ways to be more productive is to do goal-setting each day. This practice is so powerful that I encourage you do it for each work activity, too. For ex-ample, if you're calling a co-worker, take a few seconds before the call to identify the goal. Odds are, the call will be more efficient and meaningful rather than random and purposeless. When you hang up, you'll immediately know whether or not you hit your target. Likewise, if you're planning to have an important conversation with your boss, get clarity around your goal and know it well. Since most of us don't usually meet with our bosses to simply have "nice chats," establish a specific objective for each meeting. This improves communication overall and may even boost the odds of getting whatever you wanted.

In Summary: The Disciplined Leader is a guardian of personal time and the time of others. Defining "What's the goal?" before taking action will save time and also form greater direction and improve execution. Drive this habit through your organization, and employees will be more productive, goal-oriented, and results-focused.

Take Action!

✓ In an upcoming meeting in which you're taking the lead, define the meeting's goal. Distribute an agenda in advance, so people can be more prepared.

✓ Over the next month, look for opportunities in which you can coach your direct reports to ask "What's the goal?" around their own activities.

✓ Examine your activities by asking "What's the goal?" Discontinue whatever has no value or purpose.

Stay the Course

Disciplined Leaders know good execution is vital to their success. They have to be good at it, but they also have to find ways to get the entire organization to execute well, too. Why? If their team can't execute, they are not going to accomplish whatever they have set out to do.

MAP drives this point home with its clients by showing a scene in the movie *Hoosiers*. It provides a classic example of how staying the course and executing against a predefined strategy can make or break success. In this scene, a key player takes over the basketball game, totally disregarding the coach's strategy: pass the ball four times before you shoot. The star player sinks shot after shot, overlooking his teammates' role in the game and undermining the coach's instructions. Believing in the discipline of sticking to his strategy, the coach benches the star player and refuses to let him rejoin the game even when another team member fouls out. There, the star player sits off court while the others play on with the disadvantage of only four team members.

As outlined in this example, execution is rooted in discipline—the regular, consistent practicing of a predefined strategy that improves someone or something. Yet when the going gets tough in the implementation phase, some leaders quit their carefully crafted strategy and change course. In fact, one of MAP's national business surveys revealed 70 percent of responding CEOs felt their strategies were the right ones. Yet only 10 percent of respondents said the strategies were being correctly executed due to various business challenges. The implication? They experienced varying degrees of organizational failure, and that was a direct consequence of their inability to execute strategies. Occasionally MAP clients have started implementing the MAP System and then discontinued it for another management program, only to find that changing course undermined their best intentions. Only when they returned to MAP and stuck with the program did they experience real results. In fact, once back on course, a recent client transformed his business from a $2 million to an $18 million company in four years.

This point highlights the reality that challenges will invariably occur whenever you pursue a new strategy. For example, when you undertake various tactics to support the strategy and those tactics don't deliver as planned, you can be tempted to drop the strategy altogether. But when it comes to executing strategies, the difference between success and failure is how you face such obstacles and stay fearlessly focused on your vital goal. Moreover, your job as a leader for your organization is to sponsor key strategies by leading through example. Your demonstrated commitment will help align employees to the strategy you are implementing. In fact, the best leaders stay maniacally focused and avoid the temptation to get distracted because they know if they get distracted, their people will get distracted, too. Here's how to further support your ability to stay the course:

Expect rough waters. Simply having a "just do it" attitude when implementing a new strategy and then expecting smooth sailing can get you in trouble. In fact, it's downright naïve to think you can institute new directions, policies, or procedures without some troubles along the way. Problems will pop up. People will struggle. You'll possibly even doubt the direction your-self. Expecting all this is the first opportunity for managing these temporary roadblocks with courage. Better yet, develop a contingency plan of attack that anticipates any and all things that could go wrong with the new strategy. Doing so beforehand, in quieter times, surely beats developing an on-the-fly contingency plan when the problem hits.

Surface and manage resistance. Resistance to change is a normal human behavior. Expect it. When it comes to understanding what your direct reports, teams, or anyone else tied to your organization are struggling with regarding change, the best approach is to establish and maintain an environment in which you can easily uncover the concerns and issues. How do you do that? Ferociously foster open lines of communication through a candid workplace culture. Demand feedback from your team, direct reports, and even customers, so there's genuine understanding and transparency. Listen carefully to concerns and fears—then address them. When people feel like they're truly being heard and that they matter, they're more likely to stay the course with you.

Create ownership in solutions. Whether the strife is internal or external, turn to your people for the answers. Having them develop solid solutions will not just create ownership and that important buy-in but may spark creativity and innovation. All this can be very powerful, motivating your people to keep the strategy's integrity intact, so it is effective and eventually yields results.

In Summary: The Disciplined Leader knows developing an organization that executes successfully requires the discipline to stay the course on a new strategy. This means remaining focused on vital goals, avoiding distractions, and effectively managing any resistance that could derail success.

Take Action!

✓ Develop a one-page company plan that lists your agreed-upon strategies and share and monitor progress with your team.

✓ Limit ideas and strategies that your organization can effectively implement.

✓ Develop a contingency plan for anything that could go wrong and have it ready.

Lead from the Front

The Disciplined Leader must inspire others to achieve goals and support the leader's vision for success. It's a strategy that every leader must execute to ensure he or she is focused on and delivering in relationship to The Vital Few.

But what exactly do I mean by someone who inspires? I'm certainly not talking about a leader who has loads of energy. And I'm not alluding to a boss who is emotional or charismatic, per se. In fact, some of the best leaders I've worked for weren't very emotional or naturally charismatic at all. However, what they did consistently demonstrate was a passion for the business, their organization, and their team by being front and center. Whether times were good or bad, these leaders remained visible and engaged in the process. Like committed captains of a ship, they had the wisdom to know that if they hid from the storms or were detached from their crew, the consequences would be detrimental.

Just like these leaders, employees are watching to see how front and center you are. Even if they don't verbalize it, they're paying attention to your level of engagement with them and with the organization as a whole. Remaining front and center is how you can demonstrate and accomplish those objectives. Creating greater discipline around this practice will build consensus and win your employees' critical respect and loyalty. Ultimately, this leadership discipline will inspire others to achieve goals.

Here are several ways to step up and remain front and center:

Get consensus. Some years ago, MAP signed on with a new client in the food industry and quickly learned company leadership was conducting all its business, including meetings, out of their home office. Right off the bat, their MAP consultant told its co-leaders that being more front and center would be a requirement to successfully implementing the MAP System and achieving their vision of success. With MAP on board, big changes could happen. But if they were holed up in a home office all the time, out of sight yet trying to transform an organization, their efforts would fail. As difficult as it was for the business's partners, they started attending MAP's accountability meetings, which forced them to get face to face with other management in the company.

As a result, they got more engaged in their business. Doing so proved transformative. By becoming front and center, these leaders supported team relationships and grew trust. Their presence and engagement also enabled these leaders to communicate more effectively, gain consensus for their vision, and drive critical changes. They implemented MAP's accountability system by starting Vital Factor meetings. Today, that company has gone to a whole new level, having grown into a thriving regional chain that employs 3,000 people and executes the MAP program all the way down to the store level.

To execute strategies and achieve goals, you will need buy-in from your team and the organization at large because you can't achieve it alone. Be proactive about how you do this.

Lead in crisis. No one likes to think about national tragedies. But they happen, and when they do, it's make or break time for the leaders working wherever those tragedies take place. Think about the Boston Marathon bombing of 2013. What did the city's mayor do? Well, he wasn't hiding in fear. He didn't abandon ship. In true leadership form, the late Thomas Menino, who was recovering from a personal injury at the time of the bombing, signed himself out of the hospital and put himself front and center of the aftermath activity. He got to work healing and fighting for the community. That day, if people didn't love him already, he won the hearts of many and set a stellar example of how to rise to the challenge with grace. He was clearly present, invested, and involved in demanding resolution.

There may be times in your professional career when you have also had to deal with a crisis at work. Remember, your responsibility in leading your organization is to be front and center because people are relying on you. Whether the problem is big or small, consistently see the issue through until it is resolved. It's a basic expectation of your leadership job.

Sponsor change. As you've learned, resistance to change is a natural human emotion. In fact, leaders often fail at new initiatives and transitions. It's not because they don't believe in them but because they get push-back from their employees who are struggling with issues about what's been proposed and how to deal with whatever it entails. However, the onus is really on the leader to sponsor it, taking a more proactive approach by getting front and center of the change from the get-go. Employees need to see their leader's passion for it from the start, and that person in command must remain present and involved in the change itself, educating people about why it is taking place, modeling any expected change, enthusiastically talking about results, and rewarding those who both embrace and do well with it.

In Summary: The Disciplined Leader accepts that a leadership journey will include defining moments when leadership must be front and center. Seize these opportunities to fearlessly demonstrate commitment to your values, people, and organization. Your passion, attitude, and actions can build buy-in, greater commitment, and support from your team and the entire organization alike.

Take Action!

✓ Recognize your responsibility to create consensus and support for your company's vision. Participate in the process and lead communication efforts to support the initiative.

✓ Be front and center with change initiatives you are managing. Use all communication vehicles (face-to-face, phone, email, meetings, etc.) to raise your visibility and get your message out.

✓ Be a student of great leaders. Whether it's a president like Abraham Lincoln or a CEO like Jack Welch, examine those who've successfully led from the front and adopt best practices.

Learn From Success

Without a doubt, the value of learning from your mistakes is a lesson worth embracing, both in your personal and professional life. In leadership, it gives you a chance to take the corrective actions that can lead to sizeable victories. But after a big win or achievement, it's equally—if not more—important to pay attention to what went right and do more of whatever that is. In fact, asking what's working is one of the first questions that MAP consultants ask in their monthly accountability meetings with their clients.

With one particular client in the software industry, the CEO discovered the power of learning from a victory after he hired the right person as his company's COO. Prior to hiring the right candidate, the CEO made a toxic hire in the COO position. After too many years of struggling with this person's failure, he realized he had made a hiring mistake and that he should have fired him sooner. When he finally did fire the COO and hired the right candidate, the company's revenues exploded, and the employee base quadrupled in three years. Noting the reward of surrounding himself with the right talent, he got proactive about hiring the right people for other positions. Today, that same strategy still plays a major role in the company's continued growth and profitability.

For me, it has always been easy to spot where I went wrong as well as every little thing that contributed to my failures. If a person brought up a failure of mine, I could give a complete dissertation on all the mistakes that contributed to the problem from beginning to end. But that was not the case with my successes. When someone asked me how I did something right or well, my thoughts would get cloudy. For some reason, it was harder for me to think clearly about what specifically brought about that winning result. As a fallback, sometimes I'd say I just got lucky—the stars aligned, and good things came out of that.

But as I matured as a leader, I realized that success isn't an accident. It's really about cause and effect and, in particular, the consistent use of the very mindsets and habits this book presents. Success is also about looking closely at your victories to see how those disciplines tied to those victories have ultimately driven results. Moreover, success is a gift in so many ways—one that should never be taken for granted. With every accomplishment, big or small, there's a wealth of wonderful information that can be applied toward future actions and behaviors to boost your odds of even greater success. And it's not just about avoiding your mistakes.

One of the ways to learn from prior success is to shift your organization's attention away from trying to avoid mistakes and a bit more toward replicating success. That starts with identifying wins and taking inventory of what was done right to contribute to the outcome. Employees have their own talents, gifts, and hard-earned skills. Considering these attributes and other factors influencing your ability to succeed, the onus is on you to apply this learning to future challenges and generate even more wins. Here's how you can start:

Embrace a positive outlook. Small successes count toward something. Over time, organizations can win big by paying attention to lots of small victories. Victories will boost your confidence. Possessing self-confidence shapes decisions, behaviors, and actions for the better. The positive will attract the positive, generating success and garnering confidence. Then this positive outlook becomes a self-propelling cycle—when confidence is part of the culture, good things tend to happen, and successes of all types and sizes become the reward.

Analyze successes. As the Olympian "Athlete of the Century" Pelé once said, "Success is no accident. It is hard work, perseverance, learning, studying, sacrifice, and most of all, love of what you are doing or learning to do."

Success happens for good reasons, and when you start to explore the who, what, where, when, and why of an achievement, you'll most likely see it wasn't just some matter of pure luck. More likely, it resulted from having grit, the right approach, and the right team on board. In making a concerted effort to recognize what works, you'll now be able to apply that lesson for creating more future success. This practice will save the organization potential time, energy, and other resources by not re-inventing the wheel every time a new initiative starts. You'll have a greater, more grounded understanding of what works and what doesn't—possibly a perfect formula for securing more future victories.

Pay more attention to what works. As mentioned, I was guilty of focusing mostly on my mistakes. Perhaps you are your own worst critic, too—someone who is eager to dwell on your shortcomings or failures, overlooking all that's good and right. Why are we like this? Perhaps it's just how some of us were raised, or maybe the mindset comes from some message society imposes on us every day. Whatever the reason, dwelling on mistakes does no one any good. Find ways to note what's working well in work and life, leveraging whatever you learn to maximize your chances for more wins.

In Summary: The Disciplined Leader knows when to recognize mistakes but, more importantly, knows greater return comes from focusing on successes and not taking them for granted. Take the time to analyze what was done right and how it contributed to success, applying all lessons to future opportunities, and stop dwelling on failures.

Take Action!

✓ Understand your company's culture around victories and create a process to recognize and celebrate wins.

✓ Develop a lessons-learned process where you evaluate outcomes from major initiatives and capture the lessons learned and memorialize them.

✓ Understand your own biases and style around celebrating victories and then take corrective action if necessary.

Put More Weight on "Why?"

I have talked about how asking "why" questions can be a powerful tool for growth and development. As human beings and as a society, we are naturally wired to focus on the "how" to do something in all we do. Determining "how" is a survival skill ingrained in our very being from the time we are young. Figuring out how to do certain tasks that get results is what enables us to learn what's required for meeting essential and nonessential needs.

But interestingly, young children ask "Why?" all the time. They're genuinely curious and have this untainted thirst for more advanced explanations that go beyond just how to do something. Yet how often do their exasperated parents or teachers shrug off answering the "why" behind their wonder? This nonresponse can enable children to quit pursuing this direction of questioning to the point they eventually get out of the habit of asking. So it's not surprising many of us, who were once very curious children asking "Why?" all the time, have gotten out of practice. We've become immune to the importance of asking this question.

When I was in school, I spent considerably more time learning the "how" instead of the "why," particularly in subjects like math and English. Apart from a psychology class, discussions rarely allowed for more complicated levels of questioning. Exploring "why" was considered a time waster or irrelevant to the goal. The model for education just didn't invite that thinking or level of understanding.

But I've since learned that asking "Why?" can play a major role in what you learn from life and how you approach work. Moreover, asking "Why?" in a business setting is crucial to developing your organization's potential. MAP consistently drives the "why" mindset with the leaders it coaches, explaining how it's up to the leaders to ask "Why?" and to leave asking "How?" to their managers.

One of the biggest differentiators between managing and leading is that managers focus on the "how" while leaders focus on the "why." This is often a challenging concept for new MAP clients. Many of them started their businesses from the ground up and then grew it into something much larger. Along the way, they mostly managed everything by themselves, even if they hired a manager. Consequently, they have become a Super Manager—a big red *S* is practically emblazoned on their chest. Furthermore, they feel stuck in this role, an oppressive situation that must change to elevate their organization and achieve greater, sustainable results. Part of that change requires letting go of their Super Manager status, shifting their energy, efforts, and conversations more to the topic of "Why?" instead of "How?"

As you ask "Why?" more often, you'll find it improves focus on your Vital Few. It aligns with supporting your vision, creating transparency, and cultivating real answers and solutions with regard to what matters. When you get to the heart of what's vital, you will be able to make better leadership decisions about driving change, fueling performance, and developing your people.

That said, effectively asking "Why?" isn't easy—it takes self-discipline, the ability to let go of asking "How?" and sheer willpower to implement this practice. You have to be prepared to roll up your sleeves, proactively seek out those who have the answers, really listen, hear hard truths at times, and remain open to newfound realities. This might seem like hard work at times, but it's necessary for leadership and organizational growth.

This practice of asking "Why?" can become part of your strategy for learning and driving important changes. To apply that "why" question more often, use it to:

Challenge norms. Companies in the video gaming industry provide us a great example of this. Their workers operate in a do-or-die environment in which failing to constantly question the status quo can result in going bust overnight. Your organization might not be in such a high-tech, cutting-edge industry, but the point remains: just because something is the norm doesn't make it right. The healthiest organizations are those that question what's conventional so they can evolve and stay ahead of the game. They start this process by asking themselves, "Why are we doing this?" Many successful businesses have challenged the norm, such as CarMax, Southwest Airlines, Amazon, Apple, and others. You, too, can redefine a whole industry.

Challenge people. As you have learned, asking your people "Why?" is a great professional-development tool. For example, a MAP client in the construction industry missed his goal. When his consultant asked, "Why did you miss your goal?" the answer was "I don't know." Not good enough. The consultant drove deeper. "Why?" And the real answer was "I've got too many priorities on my plate. The boss keeps giving me more things to do, so it's hard to know what's a priority."

So, too, if your employees are missing goals, asking "Why?" will shed insight into their struggles and any opportunities for growth. It will get to the root of the problem. When they respond, you must listen carefully, remaining on alert for evasive, illusive comments, as well as those that answer the "How?" instead of the "Why?" aspect of an issue.

Challenge potential. Some of the best leaders MAP has coached were highly skilled at asking "Why?" of themselves, their people, and their organization at large. But some of them also took this line of questioning one step farther and challenged the overall potential of their people by frequently asking "Why not?" For instance, when something seemed impossible, unconventional, or even too risky, these brave leaders would say, "Why not do it?" "Why not be different from every other company?" or "Why not do what's never been done before?" Inspired and fearless, their troops would consistently rally to meet their leader's call, develop breakthrough solutions, typically implement those ideas with passion and pride, and deliver big wins for the entire organization.

In Summary: The Disciplined Leader holds the power of the question "Why?" high and knows it can often initiate positive change, drive performance, develop employees, and enhance the whole organization's capacity for excellence.

Take Action!

✓ Practice asking more open-ended questions. Look for opportunities to ask these types of questions, including at least one "why?" question in the mix.

✓ Use "Why?" to challenge organizational norms. Examine tasks and activities to determine better ways to do business. Be a devil's advocate in any meeting where proposals are offered.

✓ Adopt the "why?" question as part of your coaching style. When one of your direct reports misses his or her goals, drill deeper with "why?" questions until you've got the right answer.

Cultivate Curiosity

Curiosity is a great asset for leaders who want to significantly influence their organization. You've already learned a little about the importance of being curious, specifically by asking "Why?" more often. However, being curious in general—not just through asking "why" questions—is a subject that demands more discussion.

For instance, my guess is that when you picked up this book, you were curious about the title *The Disciplined Leader* and wondered if it could help you in any way. If so, then the simple fact of your being genuinely curious has now led you to read this book, giving you a means for driving your self-development, taking the initiative to improve your capacity, and consistently implementing proven leadership habits and tools.

Curiosity is also a strategy for discovering new solutions, particularly when it comes to running businesses differently and driving better results. People take notice and appreciate it when you are authentic about your interest in them and what they say. Be "real" about your curiosity, not just going through the motions and making small talk, and this will communicate your goal is not just to know them better but learn from them, too. People love this. Employees thrive off of it. Being authentic about what you're asking shows you care and respect others. It's a solid leadership value.

Many companies capitalize on the latest technology to get ahead in their markets. But to do that, these organizations have to be passionately, almost obsessively, curious about what their clients or customers want. So it is with a MAP client that provides real-time pricing information in today's international travel industry. One of the keys to its renowned success and significant competitive advantage has been its culture of curiosity. Its team of innately inquisitive people work in an environment that encourages out-of-the-box thinking and innovation, bolstered by tactics that foster questioning, creativity, solutions, and consistently positive results.

Here are some expanded thoughts on how you can sharpen and use curiosity to your advantage:

Generate greater business innovation. Think of all the scientists who've made some of the biggest discoveries in the past one hundred years. Being curious, asking "What if?" or "What could our organization do differently?" has always been and continues to be essential to their solutions and innovations. Like a scientist, you, too, must question in such a way, particularly if you're ever going to source new possibilities for your business. Even if you think what you've got in place works fine and makes sense, forcing yourself to regularly ask the "What if?" and then exploring how things could be done differently could result in even more efficient, cost-wise solutions.

Build human connection. To get results, you need to motivate employees. That's done, in part, by building good relationships. One of the secrets to building good relationships is to express genuine interest in others. Think about leaders you know who have a great gift for connecting with you because they're really curious about what's going on with you. They don't just ask how you're doing or what's going on, but they have excellent listening skills and the ability to spot opportunities to dig deeper and ask meaningful, interesting, and insightful questions. When you interact with them, you really come to respect and trust them. This opens the door for you to share more thoughts and ideas.

Accelerate your influence. Proactively seek out opportunities to ask questions, learn more, and spot opportunities to make positive changes at your company. When people see that you ask a lot of good questions and are eager to learn more about them and their jobs, they will be more engaged in the business. When you learn what others think, you can use this information to hone strategies and set direction. Through knowledge, you will build more capacity for success, giving you a competitive advantage.

In Summary: The Disciplined Leader models curiosity. It is the personal touch that tells others they are important, and it is the catalyst for new ideas and solutions for business. Curiosity can unlock doors on how to manage the organization better by challenging norms and engaging employees.

Take Action!

✓ Be curious about how things can be done better or differently. Identify one organizational norm that could be improved. Remember: just because you have always done something "that way" does not mean it is "the way" today.

✓ Practice an inquisitive style with your coworkers and frontline subordinates over the next thirty days. Pay attention to how it impacts them, their body language, engagement, openness, and so on.

✓ Identify something you're curious about learning at work. When the opportunity arises, meet with your boss and ask for help to get you involved in that activity.

Pick Your Battles

If you're in leadership for any length of time, I can guarantee you're going to have battles to fight and wars to win. But great leaders know, as the popular country song goes, "You've got to know when to hold 'em, know when to fold 'em, know when to walk away, know when to run." Disciplined Leaders learn to pick their battles within an organization with extreme care, so they can optimize their leadership and maintain authority.

One MAP client got his organization together and directly involved his people in deciding which battles they'd choose. The company was facing about ten identified challenges. After a long discussion, everyone voted on the top three—and 80 percent of those in the room picked the same top-three battles to fight. Why? Because most realized these three battles, which amounted to approximately 20 percent of fighting, could win 80 percent of the war. In choosing what to tackle, they embraced the Pareto Principle—20 percent of activities net 80 percent of results—and this was a critical point of understanding and empowerment because this organization didn't have the resources to fight every battle and had to focus on the most important ones to win the war.

No doubt, it's a good trait to consistently have a point of view on important matters and be known as someone who is a fighter, capable of taking a strong stance when the time calls for it. But it's counterproductive to try and win every argument. For one thing, you just won't. No one wins all the time, but, as we explained earlier, it isn't always right to be right. As professional leaders, we realize wanting to win works as long as it's not taken to an extreme. You do not want to be seen as an inflexible leader in your organization, someone who doesn't value other opinions and ideas.

So how do you determine which battles to fight and which ones to walk away from? It takes experience and wisdom to get really good at deciding what to do. But to get greater clarity, revisit that all-important question: "What's the goal?" It's a great way to initially test whether it's going to support or hurt what you've determined as vital. If you discover that your goal is to fight just to fight, and you don't have a better reason for taking a strong stance against something or someone, that's a sure indicator that you should walk away—quickly—or, maybe just consider agreeing for a change.

On the other hand, if a battle is truly worth pursuing, prepare to stand up for it. Your leadership needs to reflect your ability to discern which battles aren't worth fighting as well as your fearlessness in the face of the battles that are. It also needs to demonstrate that you're skilled in how you handle yourself, the issues, and the employees you might be defending. Here are some ways to develop and sustain these aspects of your leadership style:

> **Support healthy debate.** As a leader, you should certainly sponsor spirited discussions, but be sure they are fruitful. Don't be afraid to hold a healthy debate and let the meeting take shape. However, as you have learned, establish a few ground rules, such as no personal attacks, and consider setting time limits and goals around what

the end result needs to be. Make sure to provide moderation or facilitation to keep people on track, and then encourage employees to defend their positions. Such strong discussions can actually build teamwork and cultivate stellar ideas that can lead to company profit, growth, and other rewards.

Address direct challenges to your authority. Sooner or later, your authority will get challenged by a direct report or other employees. It could happen in a meeting or perhaps at some other venue just when you least expect it. When such a situation does occur, it will definitely be a defining moment in which you must display courage and show strength. Failing to take the situation head-on can do serious damage to your power as a leader.

Go to bat for someone or something. Going to bat for someone who needs help is part of leadership. Most leaders recognize that this action is rooted in good values, including courage, one of those essential leadership traits. For example, if a direct report is being unfairly disparaged, stand up for that person. This will be one of those critical activities that can show and display your leadership power to your organization.

In Summary: The Disciplined Leader knows, from experience and from intuition, which battles to fight and which ones to walk away from. Picking the right battles will enhance your leadership power and authority within your organization. Recognize key moments where you need to fight and act with courage.

Take Action!

✓ Think up some scenarios in which your authority might get tested. Prepare responses that would demonstrate your ability to manage the situation with authority.

✓ Examine your current activities and whether you're wasting time fighting the wrong battles. Stop having those fights and address your behavior.

✓ Determine where you can sponsor healthy, heated debates, particularly in areas with subjects that have high impact or tie directly to your vital goals.

Avoid the Dangerous Gap between Good Ideas and Execution

Have you ever fallen in love with a new idea, maybe even your own idea, that seemingly held much promise but then fell apart during the implementation phase? I have seen that happen countless times in my career. Moreover, I wish I could tell you that it didn't happen under my area of responsibility, but I would be lying. When it has happened to me, I have always been left scratching my head and dealing with the aftermath of the failure.

This happens with our clients, too. Some years ago a client signed on with MAP and mentioned she had a solid business plan complete with all kinds of carefully developed ideas for her company's growth and advancement. But what had happened with that plan? Nothing. How had she executed it? She hadn't. For an entire year, it sat untouched in a drawer, demonstrating a serious gap between her good ideas and execution.

The cost to an organization in terms of time, money, and resources resulting from failed implementation can be high. It can also tax your credibility. MAP has coached many leaders around the disparity between good ideas and execution, helping them evaluate their ability to execute the new idea before pulling the trigger and trying to implement it. It's an issue that commonly comes up in the case of companies considering new acquisitions or products. Often, a new direction or addition looks like the answer to other current problems or simply a great opportunity to expand and grow. Yet unless it's aligned with the company's greater goals and the benefits outweigh the risks, the product can quickly become deadweight or the acquisition a dead-wrong decision for business.

As a Disciplined Leader, it's your job to become curious but also cautious about good ideas. That starts with discerning the ideas and solutions introduced by your people, making those hard decisions about whether to say yes or no to them. Good ideas don't mean anything unless your organization is capable of executing them. Yet leaders often jump at something new that's been proposed and overlook what's realistic, possible, and best for all involved. They're repeatedly chasing shiny objects, using all their energy and efforts, going after whatever looks good to them at the moment and not scrutinizing how that's going to diminish their resources, lessen their livelihood, and hurt the health of their organization. One of the most common reasons their teams and organizations then fail at implementing such new ideas is they're just not capable of successfully executing them.

So whenever any new concept or strategy is put on the table, assess the gap between its good intent and your team's core ability to implement and execute it. Be rigorous in your assessment, considering the time, money, and resources needed for successful execution. Following this disciplined approach will allow you to say "no" to good ideas you can't execute and focus more on those you can.

Also, keep in mind that if you and your employees have previously been incapable of implementing new ideas, you are not alone in this leadership challenge. As you now know, hiring the right employees and putting them in the right jobs leads to greater company performance, goal achievement, and results.

Assuming you've adopted this strategic habit, you're going to have bright people coming to you with lots of bright ideas—which is exactly what you want. After all, you've purposefully hired talented employees who are not just skilled workers but also formidable thinkers and idea people.

While it's important to have such talent on your staff, beware! Sometimes you need another good idea like you need a hole in your head. In many cases, the best course of action is to just say no. The trick is to keep the ideas flowing while instituting a methodology for clarifying whether or not your team or company is equipped to execute the idea. Here are some ways to do that:

Determine if the new idea aligns to core strategies. A good way to evaluate an idea is to put it up against your company strategy and mission to look for alignment. If the new idea is in opposition to strategies you're trying to implement, you should pass on the opportunity. Let's say your strategy is to provide a higher level of customer service than your competitors. But then a new cost-cutting idea surfaces, which could compromise your organization's customer-service levels. In this case, the proposed idea is in opposition to your strategy and shouldn't be undertaken.

Evaluate if you have the right people and resources. Many times implementation fails because you don't have the right people and resources to execute it. Serious consideration needs to be given to your staff's current responsibilities and what will happen if you set them in a new direction. It's also important to evaluate your team's capabilities. Sometimes, whatever is being proposed demands new skills or talents. Since your people are your greatest asset, manage that asset well.

Determine the true costs. It's easy to underestimate the true cost and time requirements to implement a new idea or the change being proposed. So before you embrace a new idea, spend the proper time conducting a formal analysis to understand the cost and time necessary for the scope of the change. Chances are, the more you dig, the more you will discover that the cost and time requirements are higher than you think. It doesn't mean you shouldn't implement the new idea, but it is important to make an informed decision based upon all the facts so you're not caught by a surprise that wreaks unintentional havoc on your organization.

In Summary: The Disciplined Leader is watchful for any gaps between a good idea and the organization's ability to implement and execute it. Knowing all the costs up front—in terms of time, money, resources and more—will equip you with the information you need when it comes time to say "yes" or "no."

Take Action!

✓ Evaluate new ideas against your company strategy, mission, and your Vital Few. If a new idea doesn't align with these important leadership and organizational factors, say "no" to it.

✓ Determine whether your team has the capability to execute the idea. If your staff is lacking in experience and skills needed for implementation, determine a solid way to bridge the gap.

✓ Work with your team to implement a formal decision-making process for new ideas. Look at time, money, and resource requirements.

Avoid the "Flavor of the Month" Syndrome

Today's best organizations know how staying focused on their key strategies drives business results. Specifically, these companies and their leaders seemingly work miracles and get big returns by consistently engaging and aligning their teams to these strategies.

On the flip side, many companies are struggling because they are afflicted by what MAP calls the "Flavor of the Month" syndrome. These organizations change direction so frequently their employees don't understand where they're going and what's coming next. It's an incredibly dysfunctional approach to both leadership and management that wreaks havoc on the harmony organizations want and deserve. It's in complete opposition to "staying the course," which, as you've already learned, goes hand in hand with Disciplined Leadership.

Here's a good example: one of MAP's clients joined a peer group that met every month. At these meetings, new speakers with the "greatest and latest" ideas presented to the peer group. After each meeting, the client would get all excited about the "groundbreaking" concept he learned and would go back to his business and immediately take steps to implement it. After a period of time, chaos ensued. Experiencing change after change, his team and the employees became confused about their priorities and the direction of the company. Following the confusion, the employees started figuring out erratic changes were becoming the norm. When frequent changes become the standard, these employees stopped getting on board with each new idea because they knew it was just the "flavor of the month." Today's news was always tomorrow's history.

After observing the negative influence these changes were having on his company, our consultant provided coaching to this leader to get him to understand the unintended consequences he was inflicting on the team and organization. This was a turning point in the client's leadership. He took corrective action to stop the behavior and end the madness. In doing so, he was then able to get his company focused again on The Vital Few, and the results started to happen.

As with this leader, it's your job to avoid getting trapped by "Flavor of the Month" syndrome. Trust in the fact that true success comes with identifying the critical measures that will drive the achievement of your strategies, goals, and, ultimately, your vision. This will provide focus, keeping you on top of what matters rather than giving credence to distractions that might undermine your carefully plotted path.

At MAP, we adopt the premise that "What gets measured gets done." Remain true to that discipline, and your organization will be one in which everyone is on the same page, engaged, and more motivated to get results.

Here are three ways to prevent "Flavor of the Month" syndrome from destroying your organization's focus:

Create consensus during planning. As part of the planning process, it's not only important to identify key strategies but also to gain buy-in for those strategies. Consensus starts with getting input from management and employees so these people become invested and have ownership in the process. Having this dialogue and getting people involved will pay huge dividends when it comes time to implement and then execute the strategies. People want to contribute, and their contribution to the process erases the chances of them feeling surprised as the strategies come into play.

Stay committed to identified strategies. Staying focused on key strategies is a critical success factor for leadership. Throughout the year, it's leadership's job to reinforce strategies by reporting results and progress, always tying those back to why it's important to the organization and what's vital. In working with over 15,000 organizations over five decades, MAP has noted that when strategies fall apart, leadership is the culprit and, more specifically, the inability of key leaders to stay true to those key, identified strategies. After all, the onus is on those individuals to sponsor the strategies adopted through what they say, what they do, and what they reinforce with their team.

Formalize decision making for new ideas. As I have pointed out, any energetic, empowered workforce will likely bring about new ideas. Generating new ideas is rarely a bad thing. As a leader, the last thing you want to do is communicate you're not interested in fresh ideas because it will stifle employee engagement and innovation. So, send the message you welcome new ideas by giving your organization a formal method for handling them. Implement a decision-making process for suggesting new ideas, something that includes how they get submitted, reviewed, and approved or rejected. Include communication loops to clarify how and why decisions are made. Most employees understand that all ideas cannot be implemented. But if you put this process in place, they'll be more likely to respect the decisions made even if the ideas do not always get adopted.

In Summary: The Disciplined Leader knows the value of staying the course and avoiding the "Flavor of the Month." Fads are cheap and plentiful, and their attraction can cause confusion, frustration, and apathy with employees—it's a surefire way for generating chaos in any organization. Successful organizations ward off this syndrome by staying focused on key strategies, building buy-in, and adopting processes that foster and manage fresh ideas.

Take Action!

✓ Have a written, documented strategic plan that clearly articulates the organization's core strategies. Communicate that plan through a structured process.

✓ Give employees this simple test: ask them to write down the organization's core strategies without consulting anyone. If you get a variety of answers, it is time to communicate the strategy more clearly.

✓ Write and distribute guidelines to encourage and assess new ideas. Guidelines should include how well a new idea aligns to the core strategies of the company.

Listen to Your Customers

In our cost-conscious society, you need loyal customers and, in most cases, that golden 20 percent will drive 80 percent of your business's profitability. How can your organization work to build greater customer loyalty? It must build loyal relationships with its customers. This means not just addressing problems or providing what the customers believe they want and need; it means listening to them and their insights. Companies must do their homework to determine what *customers* say they want and need, then develop ways to respond accordingly. As your target audience sees and grows to trust in this brand, you'll start experiencing the right kind of results. This can put your company on the path toward growing your fan base and building more loyal followers.

MAP once had a client who, in the midst of some serious strategic planning, was extremely worried about whether she was steering her company in the right direction. So she decided to survey her customers for the first time ever and discovered, much to her surprise, that the majority loved what she was doing, the degree of product quality being provided, and the direction she was currently taking her company. Had she not listened to her customers, she might have made a different, very poor decision that could have drastically damaged customer loyalty and company profitability.

It might seem a strategy for building loyal customers is commonplace, not to mention common sense. Yet research from Bain and Company, one of the world's largest management consulting firms, tells a different story. It shows that 80 percent of company executives believe their company delivers outstanding value and a superior customer experience, but only a staggering 8 percent of their customers agree with them.[9] That's a hefty percentage of companies missing the mark. Moreover, the major disconnect indicates how little these company leaders understand what customers are really thinking, feeling—and talking about. Once again, the gap in understanding is a relationship problem, making customer satisfaction difficult to achieve and customer loyalty almost impossible to sustain.

In short, customer service is not the result of simply stamping reward cards or giving discounts. That alone doesn't generate "the love." This loyalty comes from genuine relationships—those that are carefully cultivated between the customers and your organization. This comes from interactions in which the customer feels that he or she matters personally, not financially, to a business.

The strategies you develop to provide extraordinary experiences and build your loyal fan base will be unique to your business, your Vital Few, and your bottom line. But as mentioned, developing and sustaining a robust, loyal customer base starts with gaining greater visibility about what your target audience is thinking and feeling. Here are several proven tactics for doing just that:

Get feedback from your frontline employees. Soliciting in-the-trenches feedback is a must if you want to learn what customers are thinking. Talking to frontline employees can provide a more detailed, realistic picture. Make a point to connect with these frontliners and involve them in this practice of discovery. Pose the right questions and ask them how they would recommend fixing any problems. From their input, implement the best solutions, rewarding employees for their contribution to successes. After all, they know best what's working and what's not.

Talk to your customers. No matter how experienced you are in business, never make assumptions about what your customers think, feel, want, or need. If you make this fundamental mistake, the fault in your error could grow exponentially. Spending the time to research your customers can cost you as little as one percent of your operating budget. But many decisions you make can have a dramatic impact on your bottom-line profitability, so you need to get it right. From a financial standpoint, look at customer research as a priority investment, not just an incidental expense.

Conduct "quit" studies. Talking to customers who don't buy your products or services is great for understanding how you stack up against competitors. Even more enlightening is talking to customers who quit your company. As you've learned, the best way to get to the root of problem is to ask "Why?" questions. Ask customers why they're not using or buying from your business anymore. Don't complicate the study or make it a burden for prior customers to participate.

In Summary: The Disciplined Leader fully understands loyal customers drive the profitability of every business. Nurture your relationship with them. Never assume you know what these customers want and deserve. Do your homework.

Take Action!

✓ Ask your customers what the real reason is for them doing business with you—what keeps them coming back. You may be in for a surprise that pays well in terms of new information.

✓ Commit to doing a customer survey within the next six months. Focus on what drives loyalty and how your organization rates against the competition.

✓ Develop an initiative to have key managers listen to customer service calls and report observations.

Keep Customers in the Crosshairs of Decision Making

As we stated before, in many cases, 20 percent of customers drive 80 percent of business profitability. But what if you unknowingly make business decisions that negatively affect your customers or, worse, turn your 20 percent into disgruntled customers?

When issues with your customer offerings surface, the temptation can be to apply a quick fix, some sort of superficial or cosmetic change that will mask whatever has gone wrong. But customers are savvy and more sophisticated than ever. They can quickly identify when something is not working for them. Furthermore, given the nature of our globalized consumer economy, they can find a better solution in a matter of minutes. They simply have to Google it.

A great example of this happened with an online subscription service in 2011. The company decided to separate its services from one online hub into two. In some cases, it charged its subscribers an increase of roughly 60 percent if they wanted to continue receiving the exact same services they had previously enjoyed. Furthermore, it sent its subscribers an email stating,

"You don't need to do anything to confirm your membership," as if the company was doing its customers a favor, despite complicating services and raising prices. After the announcement was made, 800,000 subscribers almost instantly abandoned the company. In addition, thousands voiced their extreme disdain, weighing down hard on the company through a number of blogs and membership feedback tools.

However, faithfully keeping your customers' interests in mind can be powerful. MAP has a client in the real estate investment industry that has maintained a phenomenal track record for keeping its clients, investors, in the crosshairs of decision making. Over the years, it has consistently gathered feedback from its clients, notably by inviting them to nice dinners during which these investors could relax, talk about their ideal investment properties, communicate the results they needed, and express their expectations of the firm. The firm has religiously used information from that feedback to create alignment between decisions made and actions taken. This approach has proved so successful that this firm has averaged a nearly 20 percent return on investments and has a waiting list for new investors.

The moral of the lesson: keep your customers in mind when making business decisions. If you don't pay attention, your company can make decisions that negatively affect them. For example, if you are cutting costs or changing the system and don't consider the consequences for the customer, bad things can happen. Some of the activities that can cause trouble might include cost cutting, removing a favorite service or product feature, or changing a system tied to customer service. As a company leader, it is your responsibility to make customer-focused decisions. Good decision making on this level demands you keep customers' needs and wants in mind.

That said, it's not enough to just make good, customer-centric decisions. You should also engage and align your employees to follow your lead when they're making decisions, too. When those two strategies come together, you've got a winning formula for building customer loyalty. Strive to put customers in the crosshairs of your decision making, and good results will follow. Below are several sample activities in which it really pays to take a close look at your decisions and ask how they could affect customers:

Planning: It is leadership's responsibility to be an advocate for customers, so focus on them whenever you conduct any business planning. If you overlook the importance of this, you might find you're getting so lost in the details of the planning process that you're forgetting about your customers. Likewise, develop your strategies and actions with the customer in mind. Consider the effects of changes when making decisions on customer systems.

Goal alignment: It is common for different departments to have goals that unintentionally oppose each other. When this occurs, the quality of customer service gets sacrificed. For example, let's say your sales team relies on product quality to meet customer demand, but the manufacturing group has a cost-cutting goal that will affect the quality of the product. In such a situation, the leadership must ensure that both departments' goals are aligned to meet customers' needs.

Customer-focused meetings: How many business meetings have you attended in which your customers are never mentioned? Unless the purpose for the meeting is to talk about customers, it may be easy to overlook why you need to talk about them in the first place. But it's a great meeting habit to keep your customers visible when you're making decisions. You can do this by establishing the following ground rule for all meetings: ask, "Do we know how this will affect our customers?" This rule will circle back around to the topic of your customers' interests. Your customers will essentially be represented at the table, forcing everyone to focus on this aspect of your business. One colleague of mine went even further. In any meeting where decisions affecting customers were likely to be made, an empty chair marked "customer" was placed at mid-table. He told me people began nodding to the chair as they discussed the proposal.

In Summary: The Disciplined Leader fully grasps the responsibility to make customer-centric decisions that drive customer service and loyalty. In many companies, 20 percent of customers drive 80 percent of profits, and this core audience needs to be front and center when business decisions are made.

Take Action!

✓ Work with others in your organization to create a philosophy and guidelines for customer service. Share these items with all team members.

✓ Establish an accountability process for aligning goals between the different departments that jointly support customer needs.

✓ Find ways to learn more about what your customers want and need. Visit with your customers periodically.

Know Your Competition

Shrewd organizations know their competition. What's more, becoming an expert on your competitors is an essential aspect to your leadership. Equipped with the best information, you can get a clearer picture of where your business stands, thus helping to spot opportunities for building your customer base. When decision-making time comes, knowing your competition also empowers you and others in your organization to make solid choices and set better courses.

Don't limit competitive information to what's obvious. Dig deep to understand your competitors' people, their products, their services, what they do well, and what they don't. Plug this competitive analysis into your business plan and see how it fits against the backdrop of what's happening in your industry. This insight will better arm you to develop an offensive strategic plan that aligns with your company's goals and your leadership vision. The more you know, the more likely you'll be able to manage the effects of your competition to your bottom line.

MAP was working with a client who wanted to grow her small company's market share. She only had one major competitor—but it was a massive company. Determined to hit her goal, however, the client started hiring with the intention to build her company's market share, a process that invariably included interviewing some of the competitor's former sales-people. Through those job candidates, she learned the major competitor was planning to discontinue a particular product—a situation that would leave its massive customer base feeling burned and abandoned. By getting to know her competitor better than the competitor's customers knew their supplier, MAP's client used that information to go after that target audience. This enabled her organization to win that customer base and achieve its goals for growth.

When you truly grasp what you're up against in your field, you can seize the opportunity to proactively carve a competitive edge. It can help reveal new ways to build loyalty, grow your customer base, and better anticipate customer needs. But if you ignore or fail to get the real story behind what's going on with your competitors, your company can fall behind the competition. Here are three ways to scout out what you're up against:

> **Shop your competition.** If possible, place some calls to find out about the products, services, and incentives your competitors offer. You may discover it's beneficial to shop the competition in person, experiencing its products and services firsthand. Whichever method you use, don't just assess products and services, but pay attention to the people, pitches, teamwork, and attitudes.

> **Scout out competitors' websites.** This is a great, initial way to get a really good sense about your competition. Everything your competitors think is important or relevant usually exists on their website. Website information is real-time competitive information, readily available for free, at your fingertips. You can get a solid feel for a company's value proposition, mission, vision, and values—all of which are clues into who they are, what they believe, what they're doing, and how they're doing it.

Talk to competitors' customers. It can be tricky, but getting your finger on the pulse of what your competitors' customers are doing is always possible. One effective way is to conduct focus groups with your competitors' customers. If your category is broad and customers are easy to find, this can work great. Leadership should sponsor efforts by investing money to con-nect with and talk to your competitor's customers. The information gathered from this activity can be used to improve service offerings and develop a competitive edge.

In Summary: The Disciplined Leader recognizes no company gets ahead of competition unless they know their competition's strengths and weaknesses. Leadership needs to drive activities and invest resources to study their competition and use this information to develop a competitive advantage.

Take Action!

✓ Draw up a competitive matrix that lists the key attributes of your competitors' strengths and weaknesses. Share that information with staff members to grow their understanding of the competition and to refine the matrix with more detail.

✓ If you take a secret-shopper approach, dig deep. Don't just get surface information.

✓ Survey your competitors' clients to look for weaknesses and opportunities. If necessary, hire an outside research firm to survey your customers and your competition to discuss why customers are loyal to your competition.

Keep Ethics Strong

It seems like you can't read the news today without coming across a story of a company being investigated for illegal or questionable business practices. These practices range from embezzlement to false claims about a service to even ignoring safety concerns about a product. Whatever the ethical sin, the stakes are high for these and many other dishonest transgressions in business. The consequences can take down the entire organization overnight and, in some cases, send a person or a whole string of people to prison. When these incidents occur, there are always victims left in the wake—everyone from employees to customers, investors, and others.

It is leadership's responsibility to make sure good ethics are part of the foundation of the company. A good starting point is to use your clearly defined vision, mission, and values to provide direction to the organization. From my perspective, using company values as a guide to manage business is a sure bet. The company values are the moral compass for your employees and organization. They should guide ethical decision making for all employees, and yet it falls on leadership to make sure this happens.

As part of your responsibility to lead your organization, you are tasked with the job to engage and align employees to your company's ethical standards. That includes leading by example and behaving ethically in how you manage and create focus around your Vital Few. Your ethical actions also serve to protect your career and the integrity of the company as a whole. The following three tactics can help build that engagement and align employees and the company's ethical standards:

Develop a code of ethics. It is important for every company to define and communicate a code of ethics. These guidelines should include how ethical issues emerge and are communicated. Employees need to understand the process for raising issues. Many companies utilize an employee handbook that contains the company's code of ethics—that's a great place to list them—but you could also have them posted in a common workspace area, where people can see them on a regular basis.

You should clearly understand the code of ethics for your organization and what your role is for managing against these standards. Also, make it clear to your employees what their role in maintaining ethics is.

Develop goals that align to ethics. Since employees focus on their goals and how they are recognized, you should develop goals that measure ethical behavior. Ethical behavior measures can be a great tool for identifying when your company's moral compass is out of alignment. Don't just measure sales but also measure the satisfaction of your customers. This approach will help align your employees to ethics because many unscrupulous companies today drive sales at any cost and leave unsatisfied customers in their wake. If your customer complaints increase at an alarming level, it could signal you have an ethics problem.

Talk ethics with your people. Look for relevant stories about individuals and companies that violate ethical standards and share them with your organization. Having an open discussion about an ethical scandal outside your company can be a real teaching moment. When your employees know you care about maintaining good ethics from the top down, it sets the example for the right behaviors and honest decision making.

In Summary: The Disciplined Leader believes strong ethics, communicated clearly, are the best rudder for the company's ship in risky waters. Strong ethics protect employees, customers, and the entire viability of the company. Disciplined Leaders act responsibly in accordance with the company's values and ethics. They lead by example and intrinsically engage and align employees to the company's ethical standards.

Take Action!

✓ Conduct a meeting with your team to review and/or update (if necessary) your company's code of ethics.

✓ Review the escalation process for reporting unethical practices. Encourage employees to surface activity that is unethical.

✓ Investigate the ethical standards and practices within your industry. Apply key learnings to your organization as appropriate.

Give Back

Are you grateful? Being grateful is a behavioral style, and so much more than just the giving of thanks over a meal, in response to a gift, or a reaction to kindness. It's a position, a mind-set, a value, an attitude, and a choice. But most importantly, being grateful can be a positive influence to others by giving back and transforming the lens through which people view your organization.

Organizations that give back can build employee pride, fueling motivation for yourself and others. It can also be a lever you can pull to breathe fresh energy into the workplace and give yourself and your organization more meaning. Not every leader or organization practices giving back or incorporates it into his or her company values, yet it is a surefire way to build a stronger organization.

Many of MAP's clients have purposefully implemented programs that give back. They invest in their community, donate a percentage of profits to charities, or find other meaningful ways to give back. One organization has a very active employee appreciation program and sponsors an orphanage in Mexico.

Another puts on an annual walk-a-thon for the disabled, and a third company has an afterschool learning program that buses disadvantaged students to a safe location where they've hired a teacher to tutor and care for the children. In the case of this particular company, which also gives 10 percent of its net profit to a specific charity, the culture has totally transformed into a more motivated, highly inspired workplace—and the results from that have been seismic. Within four years, this organization went from being a $5 million company to a $20 million company.

Here are some additional ways you and your organization can give back:

Be an internal champion. Disciplined Leaders set the tone for their teams and organizations, looking for opportunities to give back in small ways inside their organization. In the book's Conclusion, I cover the extraordinary value of paying it forward and how people can benefit from sharing their leadership experience and wisdom. Look for other ways to set the tone with your team by helping people inside your organization. I have personally been moved when employees come together to support a struggling employee who needs help. For example, I've seen how their acts of kindness made a monumental difference for co-workers who were suffering from illness or tragedy. Helping someone with no direct benefit to you can be an incredibly moving experience for you and those you lead.

Get your team involved. Getting your team involved in a worthwhile cause can be the most effective team-building strategy you undertake. The initiative doesn't have to be a huge undertaking, but it should be meaningful. Teams that work together tend to stick together. It builds team pride and a camaraderie that you sometimes don't get from running the daily business.

Get your organization involved. The reason our clients' outreach programs are successful is that it's the company leaders who are heading up the efforts. Just like these individuals, look for opportunities to get your organization involved in your community, too. Leverage your influence to get others onboard with the opportunity, and you will be positioned to promote the initiative. The benefits of these types of initiatives can be huge. First and foremost, people you help through your efforts are positively influenced. Internally, it instills employee pride and reflects the company in a positive light.

In Summary: The Disciplined Leader recognizes the positive value of contributing to the local community. Organizations that give back are demonstrating their core values in the most potent way. Employees see a different side of the community, and the many thanks they receive will move their emotions and build their pride in your company. They can say, "We did that!" Your responsibility as a leader is to personally demonstrate your commitment through your actions inside and outside your organization.

Take Action!

✓ Identify some specific community activities that your organization can sponsor.

✓ Look for opportunities to create community involvement directly with your company such as internships and school visits.

✓ Reinforce and remain accountable to your commitment. Highlight on your website the ways that your organization supports the community and gives back.

Wrap-up

Disciplined Leadership isn't just about changing your ability to lead yourself and your team. It's also about securing solid strategies and executing fundamental practices that will develop and sustain your organization so you can meet goals and get sustainable results. This is your third core area of your leadership responsibility. Your organization is a key aspect of your number one asset—your people. As a leader, it's your job to invest in your organization. This means consistently managing beyond yourself and your team in a way that accelerates your leadership influence throughout the organization and with customers, those you mentor, and the general public.

Leading the organization requires effectively mining great ideas, staying the course on strategies, and making choices that will demonstrate you value your frontline employees, your customers, and the overall reputation of the organization and its brand.

The result will be a culture that's built on execution and aligned through your Disciplined Leadership. It can be infectious, affecting everything from the morale of your employees to your relationship with your target markets.

When it comes to your organization, where are you and your firm lacking? What feels misaligned, imbalanced, or misdirected? Do your employees need more support? Are you getting feedback about struggles and problems related to customer service? Is your business being perceived as unethical in the public eye, or could its image simply be better? Your answers to these questions can help you identify your "Top Three" Vital Few for Part III. Once you know what they are, record them into the *Vital Few Template* on page 7–8.

With this final set of your "Top Three" Vital Few complete, you'll now have a total of nine Vital Few in your arsenal of leadership development. Referring to the template, next whittle down that list of nine to your "Top Five" Vital Few and use that as a manageable starting point for taking action on your Vital Few. Should you decide to work on all fifty-two tips offered within the pages of the book, good for you! But know that taking on just these "Top Five"—following our guidance for corrective action under "Take Action!"—will make a huge difference in your ability to lead yourself, lead your team, and lead your organization. Take the process to heart to become the Disciplined Leader.

Conclusion

Now Pay It Forward

Your leadership path is like a present. Whether you chose the path intentionally or ended up on this journey by accident, you are receiving an opportunity that not everyone gets in life. However, with this gift of Disciplined Leadership comes a unique responsibility. We believe that responsibility is to "pay it forward," helping others grow by sharing your knowledge and wisdom. How can you share your leadership experience? By joining the ranks of countless other successful leaders who have used their lessons to help the next generation of leaders advance their own careers.

I can say my most memorable experiences as a leader haven't been about landing big deals, ensuring big mergers, or hitting some unlikely but important company target. It's been about helping people in a meaningful way, particularly helping grow those I've worked alongside or others whom I knew outside of my job. Those experiences have been and continue to be my most special memories—they reinforce why I'm here, my purpose.

So, too, you can leverage your own professional path—including its successes and failures—to support people with raw potential climb their ladder of success. Look for the right opportunities to coach others who can benefit from your wisdom and don't limit your outreach to your direct reports. Also remember, giving to others with no expectation of reciprocation is a selfless act that will someday reap rewards beyond the scope of your immediate career situation. Individuals will not only benefit from your mentorship, but you will also enhance your overall leadership. Through this noble commitment, you will create a leadership legacy that will last—if not transcend—your lifetime.

Keep your eyes peeled for people who can prosper from your guidance, whether it is a co-worker, direct report, or someone else within your organization or outside it. If you know someone outside the business who is struggling in his or her career, reach out and offer your wisdom and guidance. They might lack experience or certain skills yet clearly have innate talent or simply demonstrate great work ethic. Help them polish their talent so they are positioned to shine and have a better impact.

Also, remember to take a coach approach, mentoring in a way that empowers people to tackle their problems or challenges. If someone is struggling, perhaps having issues with the boss, share your past experiences with difficult bosses. Explain how you managed the different situations, outlining the successful strategies you employed. Also, note that coaching doesn't have to take up a lot of time to have a sizeable impact. Giving someone a half hour of mentoring once a month, listening to concerns, and sharing what you know or have experienced can be all that's needed to inspire action and results.

Finally, tap your strengths when making it a goal in life to mentor. Look within yourself and determine what you've learned, what you're good at, and what inspires you. These are your assets to share with others to then make a positive difference as they walk their professional path. When it comes to mentoring, pay it forward to people because you genuinely care about their success. And don't be surprised by your own discoveries and what you gain. You may even win a friend for life.

Ultimately, The Disciplined Leader does not shut the door upon leaving a business or profession. The Disciplined Leader is valuable to colleagues, the community, and the economy. Mentoring starts with your heart but calls upon your head to make a lasting impact. Helping others both inside and outside your organization to grow and achieve their dreams will enrich your leadership legacy. Your experience as The Disciplined Leader will live on when you share your knowledge and wisdom with the next generation of leaders. It's a way to keep acting upon what's vital, focusing on what *really* matters.

Notes

1 Statistic Brain Research Group. "Startup Business Failure Rate by Industry." StatisticBrain.com. http://www.statisticbrain.com/startup-failure-by-industry/ (accessed Dec. 9, 2014).

2 Penn State. "Americans Struggle With Long-Term Weight Loss." *Penn State News*. http://news.psu.edu/story/165117/2010/09/03/americans-struggle-long-term-weight-loss (accessed December 9, 2014).

3 Stanford University. "'You've got to find what you love,' Jobs says.'" *Stanford News*. http://news.stanford.edu/news/2005/june15/jobs-061505.html (accessed December 9, 2014).

4 Chopra, Deepak. "Deepak Chopra: The One True Key to Forgiving Yourself." *Huffington Post*. http://www.huffingtonpost.com/2014/02/10/how-to-forgive-yourself-deepak-chopra_n_4697921.html (accessed December 9, 2014).

5 *Psychology Today*. "PSYCH BASICS Procrastination." PsychologyToday.com. http://www.psychologytoday.com/basics/procrastination (accessed December 9, 2014).

6 Albert Mehrabian. *Silent Messages* (1st ed.). Belmont, CA: Wadsworth Publishing Company, 1971.

7 Tomas Chamarro-Premuzik, "Does Money Really Affect Motivation? A Review of the Research." *Harvard Business Review*. http://blogs.hbr.org/2013/04/does-money-really-affect-motiv/ (accessed December 9, 2014).

8 Ibid.

9 James Allen, Frederick F. Reichheld, Barney Hamilton, and Rob Markey. "Closing the Delivery Gap." Bain & Company, 2005. http://bain.com/bainweb/pdfs/cms/hotTopics/closingdeliverygap.pdf.

Acknowledgments

For me, writing a book has been one of those professional challenges that really pushed my comfort zone. But without a doubt, it has been one of the most rewarding experiences of my professional career. What made this such a rich experience are the people who have helped me along the way. I feel blessed to have so many talented people contribute to this book and make it a reality.

MAP's business partner Katie Roberts of Write on Target Communications deserves special recognition for her contributions to the project. Katie suggested the original idea of writing this book and inspired me to make it happen. Her talent as a writer and editor helped shape the pages of this book. Her passion for the project was contagious, and her energy helped me get to the finish line.

The knowledge in this book represents the collective wisdom and experience of all of our MAP consultants. MAP Senior Consultants Lee Froschheiser, Steve Behunin, Mike Moore, and Pepe Charles made significant contributions to the book by sharing their consulting expertise and powerful client case studies. Lee provided guidance and support when I needed it most. I want to thank all the employees at MAP who serve our clients and made this book possible.

Neal Maillet, Editorial Director for Berrett-Koehler, has displayed enthusiasm and energy for this book from the beginning. Neal provided needed direction on the book's premise and overall framework. His excellent coaching and follow-up kept the project moving forward.

Susan Williams provided me guidance and support that took the book from a concept to a real project. Her consulting expertise and experience in the book publishing industry filled a major gap for MAP.

Roger S. Peterson, Founder of Roger S. Peterson Communications, provided editing work that solved some tough issues I encountered. His experience and expertise dramatically improved the quality of the book.

MAP'S leadership team of Kimberly House, Wendi Foxhoven, Tim King, and Kearv Seang provided me much needed support and encouragement throughout the project. Kearv effectively managed the book proposal process and important book project activities.

Allan Hauptfeld, President at Vantage Research and Consulting, Inc., conducted market research for the project and was a trusted advisor for me on this project.

I want to thank my parents, John and Margaret Manning, for having faith in me and helping me believe in myself.

Last, but certainly not least, I thank Robin, my wonderful wife, for her constant love and support throughout the process of writing this book.

Index

About the Author

John Manning is the President of Management Action Programs, Inc. (MAP), a general management consulting firm based in Southern California. Since 1960, MAP has tapped its talent and expertise to help 170,000 leaders in over 15,000 organizations nationwide create breakthrough results.

John has diverse experience in business leadership, having held executive positions in Fortune 500 companies in operations, marketing, and sales. Formerly the Director of Operations for McKesson Water Products, Inc., he was also part of a leadership team that took the company national. This move made McKesson one of the third largest bottled-water company in the United States before it was later bought by Danone in 2000.

A resident of Southern California, John enjoys mentoring young professionals and entrepreneurs. An avid cyclist, John is passionate about spending time in the great outdoors. He is devoted to his wife Robin and his entire family.

About the Editor, Katie Roberts

Katie Roberts (www.katie-roberts.com) has a solid reputation in communications and media. As a television reporter, award-winning magazine editor and writer, nonprofit business alliance founder/director, and successful, freelance writer/editor, Katie's compelling, concise, and creative talents deliver results for her clients. She works and lives in Hood River, Oregon, along with her best achievements to date—her husband and two children.

About MAP

Founded in 1960, Management Action Programs, Inc. (MAP) has accelerated the growth and success of more than 15,000 companies and 170,000 leaders nationwide. One of the industry's leading management consulting and executive development firms, MAP has helped tens of thousands of top leaders accelerate their leadership and management performance.

The MAP 2.5 Day Program and proven MAP Management System™ create discipline, accountability, and goal achievement for organizations. MAP Senior Consultants set the standard of excellence in today's business world. They are former CEOs, entrepreneurs, and business leaders carefully selected based upon their extensive experience and outstanding track record of success. They serve as executive business coaches providing insight, advice, and practical tools to meet their clients' needs.

MAP provides customized solutions for individuals, teams and entire organizations across all industries. For more information: www.mapconsulting.com or (888) 834-3040.

❀ Berrett–Koehler
BK Publishers

Berrett-Koehler is an independent publisher dedicated to an ambitious mission: *Creating a World That Works for All.*

We believe that to truly create a better world, action is needed at all levels—individual, organizational, and societal. At the individual level, our publications help people align their lives with their values and with their aspirations for a better world. At the organizational level, our publications promote progressive leadership and management practices, socially responsible approaches to business, and humane and effective organizations. At the societal level, our publications advance social and economic justice, shared prosperity, sustainability, and new solutions to national and global issues.

A major theme of our publications is "Opening Up New Space." Berrett-Koehler titles challenge conventional thinking, introduce new ideas, and foster positive change. Their common quest is changing the underlying beliefs, mindsets, institutions, and structures that keep generating the same cycles of problems, no matter who our leaders are or what improvement programs we adopt.

We strive to practice what we preach—to operate our publishing company in line with the ideas in our books. At the core of our approach is stewardship, which we define as a deep sense of responsibility to administer the company for the benefit of all of our "stakeholder" groups: authors, customers, employees, investors, service providers, and the communities and environment around us.

We are grateful to the thousands of readers, authors, and other friends of the company who consider themselves to be part of the "BK Community." We hope that you, too, will join us in our mission.

A BK Business Book

This book is part of our BK Business series. BK Business titles pioneer new and progressive leadership and management practices in all types of public, private, and nonprofit organizations. They promote socially responsible approaches to business, innovative organizational change methods, and more humane and effective organizations.

Berrett–Koehler
Publishers

A community dedicated to creating
a world that works for all

Dear Reader,

Thank you for picking up this book and joining our worldwide community of Berrett-Koehler readers. We share ideas that bring positive change into people's lives, organizations, and society.

To welcome you, we'd like to offer you a free e-book. You can pick from among twelve of our bestselling books by entering the promotional code **BKP92E** here: http://www.bkconnection.com/welcome.

When you claim your free e-book, we'll also send you a copy of our e-newsletter, the *BK Communiqué*. Although you're free to unsubscribe, there are many benefits to sticking around. In every issue of our newsletter you'll find

- A free e-book
- Tips from famous authors
- Discounts on spotlight titles
- Hilarious insider publishing news
- A chance to win a prize for answering a riddle

Best of all, our readers tell us, "Your newsletter is the only one I actually read." So claim your gift today, and please stay in touch!

Sincerely,

Charlotte Ashlock
Steward of the BK Website

Questions? Comments? Contact me at bkcommunity@bkpub.com.

Certified

Corporation
bcorporation.net